U.S.A. PINTS
U.S.A. CUPS

BABIES AND TODDLERS

Edited by
Dilys Wells

Contents

This edition first published 1980 by
Octopus Books Limited
59 Grosvenor Street, London W.1.

ISBN 0 7064 1250 8

Produced and printed in Hong Kong by
Mandarin Publishers Limited
22a Westlands Road, Quarry Bay

Weights and Measures

All measurements in this book are given in Metric, Imperial and American.

Measurements in weight in the Imperial and American system are the same. Liquid measurements are different, and the following table shows the equivalents:

Liquid measurements

1 Imperial pint	20 fluid ounces
1 American pint	16 fluid ounces
1 American cup	8 fluid ounces

Level spoon measurements are used in all recipes.

Spoon measurements

1 tablespoon	15 ml
1 teaspoon	5 ml

When preparing the recipes in this book, only follow one set of measures – they are not interchangeable.

INTRODUCTION

For the first few months of life a mother's own milk is the perfect food for her baby. Some years ago it was fashionable to start mixed feeding at a very early age. Many babies were given solid food, usually a little cereal mixed into their evening bottle of milk, when they were only a few weeks old. Unfortunately, many of these babies became overweight as a result and nowadays it is considered healthier to delay mixed feeding until the baby is at least four months of age. Human milk, or baby milk powders formulated to resemble mothers' milk as closely as possible, contain the right balance of nutrients for a baby to double or even treble his birth weight. But there comes a time, usually between four and six months of age, when a baby who is growing rapidly, and becoming more active, needs the nutrients from other foods in addition to those from milk.

Enriched baby cereals with their bland, milky flavour are popular as first weaning foods. They are readily accepted and help to overcome the first hurdle in the gradual transfer from breast and bottle to spoon feeding. However, cereals should be given in small quantities only as they have a fairly high calorific value. Nutritionists advise giving babies puréed fruits and vegetables which contain iron and vitamin C, the two nutrients which are in short supply in milk. Bone and vegetable broth, puréed in a blender with lightly cooked vegetables and tender, lean meat, poultry or white fish provide a wide variety of savouries to give a baby a growing taste for solid foods. Yogurt, mild cheese, tender liver and kidney, and egg yolk are other excellent foods for babies from six months old.

To begin with, a young baby finds it difficult to swallow food from a spoon. He is used to having milk squirted to the back of his mouth. He hasn't yet learned to use his tongue, as older children do, to transfer food from the front to the back of his mouth for swallowing. If he appears to spit out everything to start with, this doesn't mean that he dislikes the food he is given. He just needs a little practice to learn to swallow.

To avoid confusing a young baby, introduce new foods slowly. Offer a small taste of a new food to begin with and then offer a little of the same food at different meals over the next few days. This helps a baby to become familiar with one food at a time and to build up his confidence in the new method of feeding. Generally, it is better to give the solid food first and finish with the breast or bottle feed. But if a baby is very hungry or distressed, it does no harm to reverse the procedure once in a while. If he does react unfavourably to one particular food, don't insist that he eats it. Offer the same food again a few weeks later. There is a greater chance of his liking it at a second try if no fuss is made at his first rejection. This is also true for toddlers and even older children. Making a child eat something he obviously doesn't like does more harm than good. After all, most

CHICKEN FRICASSÉE *(page 47)*
(Photograph: British Poultry Meat Association)

people have their special likes and dislikes and babies and toddlers are no exception. Fortunately we don't rely on any single food as a source of essential nutrients, and an attractive and well-varied diet usually provides all the nutrients required. If a child doesn't like one food, there is usually another with similar food value.

Although many babies take more readily to sweet foods, such as yogurt and mashed banana, it would be a mistake not to persevere with the less popular savouries. In fact one of the best guidelines to successful infant feeding is to encourage a baby to prefer savoury foods to sweet ones. Savoury foods, such as vegetables, meat, fish, cheese, eggs and poultry, are good sources of proteins, minerals and vitamins. Many sweet foods, such as cakes, cookies and chocolate, have a high calorific value but comparatively low protein content. Although most children enjoy sweet foods, these should be given in moderation as the sugar blunts small appetites for the more nourishing savoury foods.

From one year of age, most babies can join in family meal times, eating much the same food as older members of the family, with the exception of highly spiced or highly flavoured dishes, very rich or fatty foods, and those with a coarse texture. Many family dishes can be strained, sieved, minced or chopped for the youngest member of the family, depending upon his age and the number of teeth he possesses! An electric food blender, chopper or liquidizer is an excellent investment when there's a baby in the house. Many mothers find that an inexpensive Mouli-légumes (food mill) is quite adequate, while a small nylon sieve is the most economical of all for preparing baby food. While we suggest a blender, you can use the equipment of your choice when instructed to purée foods in the recipe section. The simplest way to purée solid and liquid foods together is with an electric blender or food processor. If you are using a hand blender such as a Mouli-légumes (food mill) or sieve, purée the solid food alone, then add enough of the liquid indicated in the recipe to make a purée of the right creamy consistency. Babies vary in the consistency of food they like. Some with no teeth at all prefer food lightly mashed, while other older children will not tolerate a single lump. Again, it's a question of individual taste.

Adults do not always appreciate that children's appetites vary from day to day. The size of a child's appetite depends, for one thing, on how fast he is growing. During the first year of life a child increases his length at birth by an average of fifty per cent. After one year of age, growth rate slows down a little, but even so, the average two year old has achieved half his or her final adult height. The faster the growth rate, the more the baby or child will want to eat.

Appetite also depends upon the amount of exercise the child takes. A baby who is kept in a playpen or pram will use less energy than one who is allowed to crawl about at will. An older child who spends the afternoon watching television will use less energy, and need less food, than one who spends the same time romping in the garden. Because children vary in the amount of food they need, we cannot be too precise about portion sizes in the recipe section.

Younger babies will usually, but not always, need less food than older ones. Parents should be guided by their own children's appetites and adjust the size of servings accordingly. However, when appetites are small, it is very important that the savoury foods are eaten first.

Many children are strongly influenced by the appearance of food. They may not like to see their food awash with quantities of gravy or sauce. All white or all brown foods, or different foods mashed together, rarely look appetizing. When a baby is first introduced to solids, tiny portions of different foods, such as lean meat and vegetables, may be puréed together for convenience, but as the baby sits up and takes notice of what he is eating, it is better to purée and serve different foods separately. Children's food should always be nicely presented and attractively served. Small appetites may be reduced still further by a plate piled with food. Small appetites need small portions, and it is much better for a child to ask for a second helping, than to have to work his way through mounds of food he does not want.

Many children do not want to eat if they are over-tired or over-excited. Long intervals between meals can mean that a child becomes excessively hungry and may be unable to eat sufficient food to provide the nourishment he needs at one large meal. Most children find that three regular meals during the day suit them best of all: breakfast, a mid-day meal, and then tea or supper. Although many adults eat only a light breakfast, this is an important meal for children who may have eaten their last meal 14 or 15 hours previously. They need to be 'topped up' with protein and energy with a well-balanced breakfast, based perhaps on milk and cereal, with a little bacon. A boiled egg with toast makes a good breakfast for older children.

The main meal dishes in this book have been chosen to suit all members of the family – mother and other adults who may be at home at mid-day, as well as the youngest six to twelve month old and toddler in the family. Unless stated otherwise, the quantities will serve two adults and two children. A suitable portion should be puréed for a baby aged six months to one year and chopped for a child over one year of age. Many of the recipes are the 'all-in-one' kind, which don't involve lots of pans and cooking utensils, and which can be served with either salad or a cooked vegetable for a complete meal. For babies under one year old, the soups included in

this book make excellent savoury meals.

Many children are not fond of cooked vegetables. This may be because vegetables develop a stronger flavour or a rather slimy texture on cooking. The non-vegetable eaters may be more enthusiastic about salads, so several suggestions for main meal salads are included. Grated vegetables, or vegetables cut into matchsticks or dice, can also be served as a side salad with a cooked main course, or be served with cottage or mild grated cheese for tea.

Keep an eye on babies and young children whenever they are eating raw fruit or vegetables. They could get into difficulties if they bite off more than they can chew.

Although many adults enjoy dinner in the evening, most young children are tired and hungry long before this, so most families prefer the children to have a tea meal at about five o'clock. Many suggestions for this meal have been included. The day's meals can end for the younger children with a milk drink at bed time.

With three good meals a day, there should be no need for children to eat between meals, though drinks may be very welcome at mid-morning and mid-afternoon. If they become very hungry, fruit, dried fruit or cheese make the best between-meal snacks. Cookies, cakes, sweets, candies and chocolate eaten between meals can have a harmful effect on developing teeth, and certainly children should not be encouraged to eat them. Many parents find sweet eating in general a vexed question. The problem is best solved by allowing children to eat a few sweets after tea, shortly before the teeth are well cleaned at bed time. However, if parents have been successful in fostering a savoury rather than a sweet tooth in their children, the sweet eating problem may never arise.

In all aspects of life, children learn from their parents, other adults and older children. They learn about food by sitting down to eat with their families and friends, and they are greatly influenced by what they hear and see. Family attitudes to food, family likes and dislikes, even the amount generally eaten at each meal, are some of the food habits a child picks up at a remarkably early age. These food habits influence his food choice throughout his own adult life. If meal times are relaxed, happy occasions when everyone enjoys eating an attractive well-balanced meal, the chances are that a young child will develop good eating habits which will lay down the foundations for a lifetime of good nutrition.

> When cooking for a baby or toddler it is very important not to add salt to savoury foods even though the food may appear bland or tasteless to an adult's palate. Babies' kidneys cannot excrete surplus salt, and salty foods can be harmful. If the baby is to share food with the rest of the family, cook without salt, remove the baby's portion and then add seasoning to the remainder to suit family taste.
>
> If fruit dishes should cause any digestive upsets, sieve all fruit for babies less than 1 year old.

SHISH KEBABS *(page 34)*
(Photograph: New Zealand Lamb Information Bureau)

BABY FOODS

Meat and Vegetables

METRIC/IMPERIAL
25-50 g/1-2 oz lean roast meat (chicken, lamb, beef or pork from the family roast), chopped
50-75 g/2-3 oz freshly boiled vegetables (mixture of carrots, peas, beans, swedes, or any green vegetables from the family meal), chopped
2-3 tablespoons thin gravy or stock

AMERICAN
1/4 cup chopped lean roast meat (chicken, lamb, beef or pork)
1/4 cup chopped freshly boiled vegetables (mixture of carrots, peas, beans, rutabaga, or green vegetables from the family meal)
2-3 tablespoons thin gravy or stock

For babies aged 6 months to 1 year: purée together the meat and vegetables, adding enough gravy or stock to make the right creamy consistency.
For children aged 1 to 2 years: chop the meat finely and mash the vegetables with a fork. Moisten with a little gravy.
Serves 1

Fish and Tomato

METRIC/IMPERIAL
25-75 g/1-3 oz poached white fish, flaked
1 tablespoon mashed potato
flesh of 1 tomato or 1 tablespoon tomato juice
1-2 tablespoons fish poaching liquid or milk

AMERICAN
¼ cup flaked poached white fish
1 tablespoon mashed potato
flesh of 1 tomato or 1 tablespoon tomato juice
1-2 tablespoons fish poaching liquid or milk

Check that all the bones and skin have been removed from the fish.
For babies aged 6 months to 1 year: purée together the fish and vegetables, adding sufficient liquid to make the right creamy consistency.
For children aged 1 to 2 years: flake the fish and serve with the potato and chopped tomato.
Serves 1

Liver and Beans

METRIC/IMPERIAL
1 chicken liver or 25 g/1 oz chicken liver
4 tablespoons chicken stock
½ teaspoon tomato purée
2 tablespoons baked beans in tomato sauce
2 tablespoons mashed potato

AMERICAN
1 chicken liver or 1 oz chicken liver
¼ cup chicken stock
½ teaspoon tomato paste
2 tablespoons baked beans in tomato sauce
2 tablespoons mashed potato

Wash the chicken liver and place in a small pan. Add the chicken stock and tomato purée (paste). Heat gently to simmering point, cover and simmer gently for 7 minutes.
For babies aged 6 months to 1 year: purée together all the ingredients, adding sufficient stock to make the right creamy consistency.
For children aged 1 to 2 years: mash or chop the liver and serve with the vegetables. Moisten with a little stock.
Serves 1

Creamed Roes

METRIC/IMPERIAL
100 g/4 oz soft herring or cod roes
6 tablespoons milk or baby milk
1 teaspoon cornflour
little milk

AMERICAN
1/4 lb soft herring or cod roes
6 tablespoons milk or baby milk
1 teaspoon cornstarch
little milk

Rinse the roes in cold water. Put the roes and milk in a small pan, cover and simmer for 5 to 10 minutes. Mash the roes in the milk with a fork, or put through a hand blender, and return to the pan. Blend the cornflour (cornstarch) with a little cold milk and stir into the mashed or blended roes. Bring to boiling point, stirring, and simmer for 5 minutes.
For babies aged 6 months to 1 year: serve with green vegetables puréed in a blender.
For children aged 1 to 2 years: serve with finely chopped green vegetables and a little mashed potato.
Serves 1

Cottage Cheese Custard

METRIC/IMPERIAL
1 egg (yolk only for babies aged 6-8 months)
2 tablespoons milk
2 tablespoons cottage cheese

AMERICAN
1 egg (yolk only for babies aged 6-8 months)
2 tablespoons milk
2 tablespoons low fat cream cheese

Beat the egg (or yolk) with the milk. Sieve (strain) the cottage cheese (low fat cream cheese) if the custard is for babies under 8 months old. Blend the cheese into the egg and milk. Lightly grease an individual soufflé dish or casserole. Pour in the egg mixture. Cover with foil. Stand in a small baking tin and pour in hot water to come halfway up the sides of the dish or casserole. Place in a preheated moderate oven (180°C/350°F, Gas Mark 4) for 20 minutes or until set.
For babies aged 6 months to 1 year: serve with vegetables puréed in a blender.
For children aged 1 to 2 years: serve with diced vegetables.
Serves 1

CHICKEN AND RICE MOULDS *(page 46)*
(Photograph: The Prestige Group Limited)

Cheese with Carrot and Tomato

METRIC/IMPERIAL	AMERICAN
1 medium carrot, sliced	*1 medium carrot, sliced*
1 tomato, skinned, or 1 canned tomato	*1 tomato, skinned, or 1 canned tomato*
1-2 tablespoons mild Cheddar cheese, finely grated	*1-2 tablespoons finely grated mild Cheddar cheese*
1-2 tablespoons boiling water	*1-2 tablespoons boiling water*

Place the carrot in a pan containing 2 cm/¾ inch boiling water. Cover and simmer until tender, about 15 minutes. Drain the carrot.

Purée the carrot and tomato in a blender, then strain through a nylon sieve (strainer) to remove tomato seeds.

Mix the finely grated cheese with the boiling water and stir until the cheese melts. Mix the melted cheese with the carrot and tomato purée.

For babies aged 6 months to 1 year: serve as prepared.

For children aged 1 to 2 years: serve with diced, boiled potatoes or with small pasta shells.

Serves 1

Apple and Rice Pudding

METRIC/IMPERIAL	AMERICAN
1 small cooking apple	*1 small baking apple*
1 tablespoon round-grain (pudding) rice	*1 tablespoon round-grain (pudding) rice*
150 ml/¼ pint milk or baby milk	*⅔ cup milk or baby milk*
1 teaspoon clear honey	*1 teaspoon clear honey*
1 yolk of egg (grade 5 or 6)	*1 yolk of a small egg*

Wash the cooking (baking) apple and remove the core with an apple corer. Cut through the skin around the centre of the apple. Place in a small pan and pour in water to a depth of 2.5 cm/1 inch. Simmer gently for 20 minutes until the apple is tender. Drain off the water. Cut the apple in half and scrape out the apple pulp.

Meanwhile, wash the rice, place in a small pan or in the top of a double boiler and add the milk. Cover the pan and cook the rice gently until tender. Remove from the heat. Mix the honey and egg yolk together, then stir into the cooked rice. Reheat gently, stirring until the mixture thickens, about 4 minutes.

For babies aged 6 months to 1 year: purée together the apple pulp and rice pudding.

For children aged 1 to 2 years: serve the apple pulp with the rice pudding.

Serves 1 to 2

Apricot Custard

METRIC/IMPERIAL
25 g/1 oz dried apricot halves
1 egg yolk
4 tablespoons natural yogurt
2 teaspoons clear honey

AMERICAN
2 tablespoons chopped dried apricots
1 egg yolk
1/4 cup unflavored yogurt
2 teaspoons clear honey

Put the dried apricots in a bowl, pour over sufficient boiling water to cover them well. Leave to stand for 2 hours. Drain the apricots, place in a small pan and cover with water. Bring to the boil, cover and simmer for 5 minutes. Drain and purée the apricots, then beat in the egg yolk, yogurt and honey. If using an electric blender, purée together the apricots, egg yolk, yogurt and honey.
Serves 1

Prune Fool

METRIC/IMPERIAL
4 dried prunes, soaked overnight
1 teaspoon custard powder
5 tablespoons milk or baby milk
1 teaspoon clear honey

AMERICAN
4 dried prunes, soaked overnight
1 teaspoon custard powder
1/3 cup milk or baby milk
1 teaspoon clear honey

Put the prunes in a pan, cover with cold water and bring to the boil. Reduce the heat, cover and simmer gently for 15 minutes. Remove the stones (pits) from the prunes.

Blend the custard powder with a little of the milk. Add the remaining milk and pour into a small saucepan. Bring to the boil, stirring, then simmer gently for 2 minutes.

If you have an electric blender, purée all the ingredients together. If not, purée the prunes in a Mouli-légumes (food mill) and stir in custard and honey.
Serves 1

Cottage Cheese and Banana

METRIC/IMPERIAL
1/2 banana, peeled
3 tablespoons cottage cheese
1 tablespoon fresh orange juice

AMERICAN
1/2 banana, peeled
3 tablespoons low fat cream cheese
1 tablespoon fresh orange juice

Mash the banana in a dish using a fork. Add the cheese and orange juice and mash or blend with the banana.
Serves 1

BREAKFASTS

Morning Scramble

METRIC/IMPERIAL	AMERICAN
1 thick slice of brown bread	*1 thick slice of brown bread*
2 eggs	*2 eggs*
1 tablespoon milk	*1 tablespoon milk*
25 g/1 oz butter	*2 tablespoons butter*
4 mushrooms, chopped	*4 mushrooms, chopped*

Cut the bread into 1 cm/½ inch cubes. Beat together the eggs and milk. Heat half the butter in a frying pan (skillet); add the bread and mushrooms and cook until the bread is golden and crisp. Add the remaining fat and reduce the heat. Pour in the eggs and cook, stirring, until the eggs are scrambled. Serve immediately.

Alternatively, cook the eggs separately, top with the mushrooms and serve with fingers of lightly toasted brown bread.

Serves 2 children

For children over 1 year old

Variations:

Use finely chopped lamb's kidney or flaked smoked fish (take care to remove the bones) in place of the mushrooms.

MORNING SCRAMBLE
(Photograph: Mushroom Growers' Association)

Summer Breakfast

METRIC/IMPERIAL
1 dessert apple, peeled and finely grated
2 tablespoons lemon juice
75 g/3 oz porridge oats
3 tablespoons wheatgerm
50 g/2 oz mixed dried fruit, chopped
1 teaspoon grated lemon rind
25 g/1 oz soft brown sugar
1 × 150 g/5 oz carton natural yogurt

AMERICAN
1 dessert apple, peeled and finely grated
2 tablespoons lemon juice
1 cup rolled oats
3 tablespoons wheatgerm
1/3 cup chopped mixed dried fruit
1 teaspoon grated zest of lemon
2 tablespoons light brown sugar
1 × 5 oz carton unflavored yogurt

Mix the apple with the lemon juice. Combine with the remaining ingredients and allow to soak overnight. Serve with fresh or stewed fruits in season.
For babies aged 6 months to 1 year: grind or blend the oats, wheatgerm and dried fruit until they are very fine.
Serves 2 children

Variations:
Use finely chopped dried apricots or peaches and apricot-flavoured yogurt.
When strawberries or raspberries are available, crush the fruit and use in place of the apple.
For children over three years, include some finely chopped walnuts or use hazelnut yogurt.

Breakfast Toasty

METRIC/IMPERIAL
1 slice wholemeal bread
15 g/1/2 oz butter
1 small tomato, sliced
25 g/1 oz Cheddar cheese, grated
1 tablespoon milk
1 rasher streaky bacon, derinded

AMERICAN
1 slice wholewheat bread
1 tablespoon butter
1 small tomato, sliced
1/4 cup grated Cheddar cheese
1 tablespoon milk
1 bacon slice

Toast the bread lightly on both sides. Spread one side with the butter and cover with tomato slices. Mix together the cheese and milk. Spread over the tomato slices. Lay the bacon on top. Place under a moderately hot grill (broiler) and cook gently until the bacon is cooked and the cheese melts and turns golden.
Serves 1
For children over 1 year old

Bacon Croquettes

METRIC/IMPERIAL
225 g/8 oz back bacon rashers, rind removed
225 g/8 oz mashed potato
1 egg, beaten
1 tablespoon freshly chopped parsley
2-4 tablespoons browned breadcrumbs
lard or oil for shallow frying

AMERICAN
½ lb Canadian bacon slices
1 cup mashed potato
1 egg, beaten
1 tablespoon freshly chopped parsley
2-4 tablespoons browned breadcrumbs
lard or oil for shallow frying

Grill (broil) the bacon until cooked but not crisp, then chop finely. Mix together the bacon and potato. Set aside 2 teaspoons of the beaten egg, then mix the remainder with the parsley into the potato mixture.

Divide into 4 portions on a floured board and shape each portion into a croquette shape. Brush each croquette with the reserved egg. Coat with the breadcrumbs. Fry in shallow fat or oil until golden brown. Drain well on absorbent paper towels. Serve hot.

Serves 2 children
For children over 1 year old

Eggy Bread

METRIC/IMPERIAL
1 egg, beaten
2 large slices of bread, cut into squares, triangles or fingers
15 g/½ oz butter

AMERICAN
1 egg, beaten
2 large slices of bread, cut into squares, triangles or fingers
1 tablespoon butter

Beat the egg in a fairly shallow bowl. Dip the pieces of bread into the egg, then lightly fry on both sides in butter.
For babies aged 6 months to 1 year: cut into tiny pieces and serve as finger food.
For children over 1 year: serve with small pieces of crisply fried bacon, grilled (broiled) kidney or black (blood) sausage.
Serves 2 children

Variations:
Cut into fingers for a child to dip into tomato sauce or ketchup; or cut into fancy shapes with a biscuit (cookie) cutter. Instead of plain bread, dip peanut butter sandwiches into the egg and fry as above. For a sweet breakfast dish, either sprinkle with lemon or orange juice or cinnamon and a *little* icing (confectioners') sugar.

Fruit and Honey Yogurt

METRIC/IMPERIAL
225 g/8 oz cooking apples, peeled, cored and sliced
25 g/1 oz seedless raisins
25 g/1 oz sugar
2 tablespoons water
pinch of powdered cloves (optional)
2 tablespoons clear honey
1 × 150 g/5 oz carton natural yogurt

AMERICAN
2 cups sliced baking apples
3 tablespoons seedless raisins
2 tablespoons sugar
2 tablespoons water
pinch of powdered cloves (optional)
2 tablespoons clear honey
1 × 5 oz carton unflavored yogurt

Put the apples, raisins, sugar and water in a pan. Cover with a lid and cook over a gentle heat until the apples are just tender. Remove from the heat and stir in the powdered cloves, if used. Leave to cool.

Blend together the honey and yogurt. When the apple mixture is cold, divide between 4 individual dishes. Spoon the yogurt and honey mixture on top. Serve cold.

For babies aged 6 months to 1 year: purée the stewed apple mixture before topping with yogurt.

Serves 4 children

Jungle Juice

METRIC/IMPERIAL
2 bananas, peeled
1 packet orange-flavoured vitamin C drink crystals
2 teaspoons honey
½ teaspoon cinnamon
600 ml/1 pint cold milk

AMERICAN
2 bananas, peeled
1 package orange-flavored vitamin C drink crystals
2 teaspoons honey
½ teaspoon cinnamon
2½ cups cold milk

Mash the bananas in a bowl. Add the orange crystals, honey and cinnamon. Gradually whisk in the milk. Pour into individual glasses.

Serves 4 children

For children over 1 year old

FRUIT AND HONEY YOGURT
(Photograph: The Tupperware Company)

SOUPS

Cream of Tomato Soup

METRIC/IMPERIAL
2 rashers streaky bacon, rind removed, and chopped
1 onion, finely chopped
1 carrot, thinly sliced
1 stick celery, finely chopped
1 × 400 g/14 oz can peeled tomatoes
750 ml/1 1/4 pints water or stock
bouquet garni
1 tablespoon cornflour
150 ml/1/4 pint milk
fingers of toasted wholemeal bread

AMERICAN
2 bacon slices, chopped
1 onion, finely chopped
1 carrot, thinly sliced
1 stalk celery, finely chopped
1 × 14 oz can peeled tomatoes
3 cups water or stock
bouquet garni
1 tablespoon cornstarch
2/3 cup milk
fingers of toasted wholewheat bread

Fry the bacon in a large pan until the fat runs. Add the onion, carrot and celery, cover and cook gently for about 10 minutes. Add the canned tomatoes, water or stock and bouquet garni. Heat to simmering point, then cover and simmer gently for 20 minutes. Remove the bouquet garni. Cool slightly, then purée in a blender and finally pass through a sieve (strainer). Return the soup to the pan.

Blend the cornflour (cornstarch) with a little of the cold milk, then stir into the soup with the remainder of the milk. Reheat to boiling point and simmer for 2 minutes, stirring continuously. Serve with fingers of toasted wholemeal (wholewheat) bread.

For babies aged 6 months to 1 year: mash tiny cubes of wholemeal (wholewheat) bread, with crusts removed, into the soup and sprinkle with a tablespoon of finely grated mild Cheddar cheese.

Scotch Broth

METRIC/IMPERIAL	AMERICAN
50 g/2 oz pearl barley	*1/4 cup pearl barley*
500 g/1 lb neck of lamb	*1 lb neck of lamb*
1 litre/1 3/4 pints water	*4 1/4 cups water*
2 carrots, diced	*2 carrots, diced*
1 turnip, diced	*1 turnip, diced*
1 onion, chopped	*1 onion, chopped*
1 leek, finely sliced	*1 leek, finely sliced*
pinch of mixed herbs	*pinch of mixed herbs*

Soak the pearl barley overnight. Remove as much fat as possible from the meat. Put the meat into a saucepan and cover with the water. Bring to the boil and skim off the scum as it rises to the surface. Cover the pan and simmer for 1 hour. Add the vegetables to the pan, together with the drained pearl barley and the herbs. Continue cooking gently for a further 1 to 1½ hours. Take out the meat and chop it, discarding the bones. Return the meat to the soup. Remove any fat remaining on the surface. Reheat before serving.
For babies aged 6 months to 1 year: purée some meat and vegetables from the soup, adding enough liquid to give a creamy consistency.

Mushroom and Chicken Soup

METRIC/IMPERIAL	AMERICAN
50 g/2 oz butter	*1/4 cup butter*
50 g/2 oz plain flour	*1/2 cup all-purpose flour*
450 ml/3/4 pint milk	*2 cups milk*
450 ml/3/4 pint chicken stock	*2 cups chicken stock*
pinch of ground mace	*pinch of ground mace*
100 g/4 oz mushrooms, chopped	*1 cup chopped mushrooms*
50 g/2 oz cooked chicken, finely chopped	*1/4 cup finely chopped cooked chicken*
1 mushroom, thinly sliced, to garnish	*1 mushroom, thinly sliced, to garnish*
toast to serve	*toast to serve*

Melt the butter in a large saucepan, then remove from the heat and stir in the flour. Add the milk, stock and mace and stir over a gentle heat until thickened and smooth. Simmer for 2 minutes. Add the mushrooms and chicken to the soup and return to the boil. Garnish each bowl of soup with a few slices of mushroom. Serve with fancy shapes cut from toast with a biscuit (cookie) cutter.
For babies aged 6 months to 1 year: strain off 1 tablespoon of the chicken and mushroom pieces. Blend with extra fresh vegetables, if available, adding sufficient soup to make the correct consistency.

Fresh Vegetable Soup

METRIC/IMPERIAL
2 tablespoons oil
2 carrots, thinly sliced
2 sticks celery, chopped
1 onion, chopped
1 potato, diced
1 clove garlic, crushed
1 litre/1¾ pints beef stock
1 tablespoon Worcestershire sauce
1 leek, sliced
4 tomatoes, skinned and chopped
75 g/3 oz green cabbage, shredded
50 g/2 oz small pasta shapes
50 g/2 oz Cheddar cheese, finely grated, to serve

AMERICAN
2 tablespoons oil
2 carrots, thinly sliced
2 stalks celery, chopped
1 onion, chopped
1 potato, diced
1 clove garlic, crushed
4¼ cups beef stock
1 tablespoon Worcestershire sauce
1 leek, sliced
4 tomatoes, skinned and chopped
1 cup shredded green cabbage
¼ cup small pasta shapes
½ cup finely grated Cheddar cheese, to serve

Heat the oil in a large saucepan and add the carrots, celery, onion, potato and garlic. Fry gently until the vegetables begin to soften. Add the stock and Worcestershire sauce, cover and simmer for 15 minutes. Add the leek, tomatoes, shredded cabbage and pasta. Simmer the soup, uncovered, for a further 15 minutes. Serve the cheese sprinkled on the soup.
For babies aged 6 months to 1 year: take 6 tablespoons of soup and purée in a blender.

Kidney Soup

METRIC/IMPERIAL
25 g/1 oz butter
1 onion, finely chopped
225 g/8 oz ox kidney, skinned, cored and chopped
25 g/1 oz plain flour
900 ml/1½ pints beef stock

AMERICAN
2 tablespoons butter
1 onion, finely chopped
½ lb beef kidney, skinned, cored and chopped
¼ cup all-purpose flour
3¾ cups beef stock

Melt the butter in a saucepan and cook the onion gently until it has softened. Add the kidney to pan. Stir in the flour and gradually blend in the stock. Bring slowly to the boil, then reduce the heat and simmer for 45 minutes.
For babies aged 6 months to 1 year: purée some of the kidney from the soup, adding a little fresh vegetable, if available, with enough liquid from the soup to give the correct consistency.

MUSHROOM AND CHICKEN SOUP *(page 27)*
(Photograph: Mushroom Growers' Association)

Green Pea Soup

METRIC/IMPERIAL
100 g/4 oz freshly shelled or frozen peas
150 ml/¼ pint water or stock
sprig of fresh mint
1 × 150 g/5 oz carton natural yogurt
1 teaspoon freshly chopped mint to garnish

AMERICAN
¼ lb freshly shelled or frozen peas
⅔ cup water or stock
sprig of fresh mint
1 × 5 oz carton unflavored yogurt
1 teaspoon freshly chopped mint to garnish

Put the peas and water or stock and mint in a pan. Bring to the boil, cover and simmer until the peas are tender, about 5 to 8 minutes. Remove the mint. Purée the peas, cooking liquid and yogurt in a blender until smooth. Alternatively, sieve (strain) the peas and mix with the cooking liquid and yogurt. Return to the pan and reheat very gently. Serve sprinkled with chopped mint.
For babies aged 6 months to 1 year: add an extra tablespoon of yogurt or sieved cottage cheese (low fat cream cheese).
Serves 1 adult and 1 child

Variations:
To make other green vegetable soups use cauliflower, Brussels sprouts, spinach or broad (lima) beans in place of the peas.

Lentil Soup

METRIC/IMPERIAL
2 teaspoons yeast extract
900 ml/1 ½ pints water
100 g/4 oz red lentils
2 carrots, finely chopped
1 onion, finely chopped
3 rashers streaky bacon, rind removed, and finely chopped
1 tablespoon tomato purée
1 tablespoon wholemeal flour
250 ml/8 fl oz milk
2 slices wholemeal bread to garnish

AMERICAN
2 teaspoons brewer's yeast
3¾ cups water
½ cup red lentils
2 carrots, finely chopped
1 onion, finely chopped
3 bacon slices, finely chopped
1 tablespoon tomato paste
1 tablespoon wholewheat flour
1 cup milk
2 slices wholewheat bread to garnish

Dissolve the yeast extract (brewer's yeast) in the water in a large pan. Add the lentils and bring to the boil; reduce the heat, cover the pan and simmer gently for 30 minutes. Add the carrots, onion, bacon, and tomato purée (paste). Reheat to simmering point, cover and simmer for a further 30 minutes.

Blend the flour with the milk and stir into the soup. Heat, stirring continuously, until the soup boils.

Toast the bread on both sides and cut into small squares to form croûtons. Serve the soup hot, garnished with the croûtons.

For babies aged 6 months to 1 year: strain some of the lentils, bacon and other vegetables. Purée in a blender with enough liquid to make a creamy consistency.

MAIN MEALS

MEAT

Beef Stew with Dumplings

METRIC/IMPERIAL	AMERICAN
1 tablespoon cooking oil	*1 tablespoon cooking oil*
1 large onion, chopped	*1 large onion, chopped*
2 sticks celery, chopped	*2 stalks celery, chopped*
750 g/1½ lb stewing steak, cubed	*1½ lb stewing steak, cubed*
50 g/2 oz plain flour	*½ cup all-purpose flour*
3 carrots, sliced	*3 carrots, sliced*
900 ml/1½ pints beef stock	*3¾ cups beef stock*
2 tablespoons tomato purée	*2 tablespoons tomato paste*
freshly chopped parsley to garnish	*freshly chopped parsley to garnish*
Dumplings:	**Dumplings:**
100 g/4 oz self-raising flour	*1 cup all-purpose flour*
50 g/2 oz shredded suet	*½ cup shredded suet*
4 tablespoons cold water	*¼ cup cold water*

Heat the oil in a pan and fry the onion and celery until the onion is soft, about 3 minutes. Remove the onion and celery from the pan. Toss the steak in the flour, then add to the pan and fry until browned, stirring frequently. Add the carrots, onion and celery. Stir in the stock and tomato purée (paste). Bring to the boil, cover and simmer for 1½ to 2 hours, until the meat is tender.

Meanwhile make the dumplings. Sift the flour, and stir in the suet. Add the water and mix to a soft dough. Shape into 8 small balls. Add to the stew 30 minutes before the end of the cooking time and cook until the dumplings are well risen. Sprinkle with chopped parsley before serving.

BEEF STEW WITH DUMPLINGS
(Photograph: Flour Advisory Bureau)

Baby Bolognese

METRIC/IMPERIAL
25 g/1 oz butter
1 small clove garlic, crushed
1 medium onion, finely chopped
500 g/1 lb minced beef
25 g/1 oz plain flour
2 tablespoons tomato purée
1 stock cube
150 ml/¼ pint water
small pasta shapes, cooked, to serve
25 g/1 oz Parmesan cheese, grated

AMERICAN
2 tablespoons butter
1 small clove garlic, crushed
1 medium onion, finely chopped
1 lb ground beef
¼ cup all-purpose flour
2 tablespoons tomato paste
2 bouillon cubes
⅔ cup water
small pasta shapes, cooked, to serve
¼ cup grated Parmesan cheese

Melt the butter in a frying pan (skillet) and fry the garlic and onion until golden. Add the minced (ground) beef and fry for 2 minutes, turning frequently. Stir in the flour and cook for a further 1 minute. Remove from the heat. Add the tomato purée (paste), stock (bouillon) cube(s) and water. Return to the heat and cook, stirring, until thickened. Simmer gently for 1 hour. Serve with small pasta shapes and sprinkle with cheese.
For babies aged 6 months to 1 year: purée a little of the meat sauce with 1 tablespoon of pasta shells, then stir in a little cheese.

Shish Kebabs

METRIC/IMPERIAL
500 g/1 lb leg of lamb, veal or pork fillet
1 × 150 g/5 oz carton natural yogurt
1 tablespoon lemon juice
pinch of dried marjoram

AMERICAN
1 lb leg of lamb, veal or pork fillet
1 × 5 oz carton unflavored yogurt
1 tablespoon lemon juice
pinch of dried marjoram

Cut the meat into small cubes. Blend the yogurt, lemon juice and marjoram. Place the meat and the yogurt mixture together in a bowl. Cover and leave to marinate for 30 minutes. Thread the meat closely together on skewers, choosing the smallest pieces of meat for the toddler's portion. (At this stage you can sprinkle the adult portions with salt and freshly ground black pepper.)

Place under a preheated grill (broiler), turning the skewers at intervals, until the meat is well cooked (about 20 to 25 minutes). Serve with jacket baked potatoes and green salad, using any remaining marinade as a dressing.
For babies aged 6 months to 1 year: purée in a blender 3 or 4 cubes of cooked meat with the yogurt marinade and a little potato scooped from the potato baked in its jacket.

Steak and Kidney in the Hole

METRIC/IMPERIAL
Meat balls:
350 g/12 oz minced beef
100 g/4 oz lamb's kidneys, finely chopped
1 small onion, grated
50 g/2 oz fresh white breadcrumbs
1 teaspoon Worcestershire sauce
Batter:
100 g/4 oz plain flour
1 large egg
300 ml/½ pint milk

AMERICAN
Meat balls:
1½ cups ground beef
¼ lb lamb kidneys, finely chopped
1 small onion, grated
1 cup fresh white breadcrumbs
1 teaspoon Worcestershire sauce
Batter:
1 cup all-purpose flour
1 egg
1¼ cups milk

Combine the meat ball ingredients and shape the mixture into 8 balls. Reserve 1 meat ball for a baby in the family and place the remaining balls, evenly spaced, in a greased roasting pan, 18 x 18 cm/7 x 7 inches. Bake in a preheated hot oven (220°C/425°F, Gas Mark 7) for 15 minutes.

Beat the batter ingredients thoroughly. Pour the batter over the partly cooked meat balls and return the pan to the oven. Bake for a further 30 to 40 minutes, until risen and golden. Serve with gravy or tomato sauce.

For babies aged 6 months to 1 year: wrap the reserved meat ball with a small peeled and sliced tomato in foil. Flatten the meat into a flat cake and bake in the oven alongside the main dish. When cooked, cool slightly, then purée the contents of the parcel.

Potatoburger Pie

METRIC/IMPERIAL
500 g/1 lb potatoes, grated
1 × 225 g/8 oz can peeled tomatoes
500 g/1 lb minced beef
1 onion, finely chopped
1 tablespoon freshly chopped parsley

AMERICAN
1 lb potatoes, grated
1 × 8 oz can peeled tomatoes
2 cups ground beef
1 onion, finely chopped
1 tablespoon freshly chopped parsley

Pour off any excess water from the potatoes. Drain the tomatoes, reserving the juice. Blend all the ingredients together and transfer the mixture to a well-greased pie dish. Cover with foil and bake in a preheated moderate oven (160°C/325°F, Gas Mark 3) for 1¼ hours.

For babies aged 6 months to 1 year: purée a little of the mixture from the bottom of the pie with some of the reserved tomato juice.

Lamb Hot-pot

METRIC/IMPERIAL	AMERICAN
100 g/4 oz pearl barley	*½ cup pearl barley*
1 kg/2 lb stewing lamb	*2 lb stewing lamb*
3 carrots, sliced	*3 carrots, sliced*
1 small swede, diced	*1 small rutabaga, diced*
2 medium onions, sliced	*2 medium onions, sliced*
500 g/1 lb potatoes, sliced	*1 lb potatoes, sliced*
1 stock cube	*2 bouillon cubes*
600 ml/1 pint boiling water	*2½ cups boiling water*
pinch of dried thyme	*pinch of dried thyme*

Cover the pearl barley with boiling water and allow to soak overnight. Trim excess fat from the lamb. Arrange the meat, vegetables and pearl barley in layers in a casserole, finishing with a layer of potatoes. Dissolve the stock (bouillon) cube(s) in the boiling water and pour into the casserole. Sprinkle the thyme on top of the potatoes. Cover the dish and bake in a preheated moderate oven (180°C/350°F, Gas Mark 4) for 1½ hours. Remove the lid from the casserole and bake for a further 30 minutes to brown the top layer of potatoes.

For babies aged 6 months to 1 year: select a lean piece of lamb, a few pieces of carrot and swede (rutabaga), and 1 small spoonful of barley. Add a little of the gravy and purée in a blender.

For children over 1 year old: serve lean meat only with a little of everything else, choosing potato slices from the centre of the hot-pot.

OFFAL (VARIETY MEATS)

Tongue and Mushroom Mould

METRIC/IMPERIAL	AMERICAN
225 g/8 oz cooked tongue, minced	*1 cup ground cooked tongue*
50 g/2 oz mushrooms, minced	*⅓ cup ground mushrooms*
1 egg, beaten	*1 egg, beaten*

Mix the tongue with the mushrooms and stir in the beaten egg. Pack the meat mixture into a lightly greased 600 ml/1 pint/2½ cup pudding basin (ovenproof bowl). Cover with foil and bake in a preheated moderate oven (180°C/350°F, Gas Mark 4) for 30 minutes. Serve hot with gravy or tomato sauce and mixed vegetables.

Serves 1 adult and 1 child

For children over 1 year old

LAMB HOT-POT
(Photograph: New Zealand Lamb Information Bureau)

Liver in Yogurt Sauce

METRIC/IMPERIAL
350 g/12 oz lambs' liver, thinly sliced
25 g/1 oz plain flour
2 tablespoons oil
1 medium onion, chopped
300 ml/½ pint stock
1 × 150 g/5 oz carton natural yogurt
4 large tomatoes, skinned, seeded and chopped

AMERICAN
¾ lb lamb liver, thinly sliced
¼ cup all-purpose flour
2 tablespoons oil
1 medium onion, chopped
1 ¼ cups stock
1 × 5 oz carton unflavored yogurt
4 large tomatoes, skinned, seeded and chopped

Cut the liver into thin strips, 1 cm/½ inch wide, and toss in the flour. Heat the oil in a large frying pan (skillet), add the onion and fry gently until soft. Add the liver and fry until the pieces are brown on all sides. Stir in the stock, then cover the pan and simmer for 20 minutes. Add the yogurt and stir thoroughly. Add the tomatoes and cook gently for a further 5 minutes until the tomatoes are just cooked. Serve with brown rice and a green vegetable.
For babies aged 6 months to 1 year: purée a small portion of liver and tomatoes with the sauce.

Mock Goose

METRIC/IMPERIAL
25 g/1 oz margarine
500 g/1 lb lambs' or calves' liver, thinly sliced
1 onion, sliced
½ teaspoon dried sage
2 eggs, beaten
350 g/12 oz potatoes, thinly sliced

AMERICAN
2 tablespoons margarine
1 lb lamb or calf liver, thinly sliced
1 onion, sliced
½ teaspoon dried sage
2 eggs, beaten
¾ lb potatoes, thinly sliced

Melt the margarine in a frying pan (skillet) and lightly fry the liver and onion for 5 minutes. Remove them from the pan and mince (grind) them finely. Add the sage and eggs and mix well. Transfer the mixture to a greased loaf tin, smooth the top and cover with the potato slices. Bake in a preheated moderately hot oven (200°C/400°F, Gas Mark 6) for 30 minutes. Serve hot with baked tomatoes or cold with salad.
For children over 1 year old

Chicken Livers in Jacket Potato

METRIC/IMPERIAL	AMERICAN
1 large potato, scrubbed	*1 large potato, scrubbed*
1 rasher streaky bacon, rind removed and chopped	*1 bacon slice, chopped*
1 teaspoon oil	*1 teaspoon oil*
100 g/4 oz chicken livers	*¼ lb chicken livers*
1 tablespoon single cream or natural yogurt	*1 tablespoon light cream or unflavored yogurt*

Bake the potato in a preheated moderately hot oven (200°C/400°F, Gas Mark 6) for 50 to 60 minutes, until cooked. Cut the baked potato in half and scoop out the centre. Mash in a bowl with a fork.

Fry the bacon gently in a small pan for 3 minutes. Add the oil. Wash the chicken livers and drain well. Chop into small pieces and add to the pan. Fry gently for 5 minutes, stirring frequently. Add the liver and bacon to the mashed potato and mix well. Stir in the cream or yogurt. Pile back into the potato jackets, heaping up. Return to the oven to heat through for 5 minutes. Serve warm with boiled green vegetables.

For babies aged 6 months to 1 year: purée a small portion of bacon and liver with some mashed potato, adding a little boiled milk to make the right creamy consistency.

Serves 1 adult and 1 child

Creamed Sweetbreads

METRIC/IMPERIAL	AMERICAN
100 g/4 oz sheep's sweetbreads	*¼ lb sheep sweetbreads*
1 tablespoon mushroom soup powder	*1 tablespoon mushroom soup powder*
150 ml/¼ pint milk	*⅔ cup milk*

Cover the sweetbreads with cold water and leave to soak for 1 hour. Drain and place in a pan. Cover with cold water, bring to the boil and boil for 1 minute. Drain and cool. Remove any skin and fibres from the sweetbreads. Return to the pan, add sufficient cold water just to cover. Bring to the boil, cover and simmer gently for 20 minutes. Lift out the sweetbreads and chop finely.

Blend the soup powder to a smooth paste with a little of the cold milk. Add to the rest of the milk in a saucepan. Heat to boiling point, stirring continuously, then simmer for 5 minutes. Stir in the sweetbreads. Serve with boiled rice and carrots or peas.

For babies aged 6 months to 1 year: purée the sweetbreads in the mushroom sauce. Serve with puréed vegetables.

Serves 1 adult and 1 child

Kidney Parcel

METRIC/IMPERIAL
1 lamb's kidney, halved and cored
15 g/½ oz butter or margarine
1 small carrot, cut into small dice
1 tomato, skinned and sliced
1 tablespoon peas, fresh or frozen
1 tablespoon water

AMERICAN
1 lamb kidney, halved and cored
1 tablespoon butter or margarine
1 small carrot, cut into small dice
1 tomato, skinned and sliced
1 tablespoon peas, fresh or frozen
1 tablespoon water

Wash the kidney well and dry on kitchen paper. Spread butter or margarine over a 5 cm/2 inch square in the centre of 30 cm/12 inch piece of foil, and place the kidney on top. Arrange the carrot, tomato and peas over the kidney, then spoon the water over. Bring two opposite edges of foil together and fold downwards twice to make a watertight seam. Fold ends of foil inwards to make a watertight parcel. Place the parcel in a saucepan of boiling water, cover and simmer for 25 to 30 minutes, until the kidney and vegetables are tender. Serve with creamed potatoes.
For babies aged 6 months to 1 year: purée the contents of the parcel with some mashed potato, adding a little boiled milk to make the right creamy consistency.
Serves 1 child

KIDNEY PARCELS
(Photograph: Bacofoil Information Service)

THE BEST OF
THE BEST OF BRITISH

POULTRY

Speedy Chicken Pie

METRIC/IMPERIAL
1 × 300 g/11 oz can condensed celery soup
150 ml/¼ pint milk
500 g/1 lb cooked chicken, diced
100 g/4 oz canned sweetcorn kernels
3 slices white bread and butter
50 g/2 oz cheese, grated

AMERICAN
1 × 11 oz can condensed celery soup
⅔ cup milk
2 cups diced cooked chicken
¾ cup canned sweetcorn kernels
3 slices white bread and butter
½ cup grated cheese

Heat the soup with the milk in a saucepan, stirring until blended. Remove from the heat and stir in chicken and sweetcorn. Turn into a 1 litre/2 pint/5 cup shallow ovenproof dish. Cut the bread into 2.5 cm/1 inch squares and place, buttered side up, on top of chicken. Sprinkle with cheese. Bake in a preheated moderately hot oven (190°C/375°F, Gas Mark 5) for about 35 minutes, until the bread is crisp and golden. Serve with French (green) beans or a tomato salad.
For babies aged 6 months to 1 year: purée some of the chicken and sweetcorn, adding sufficient sauce to give the correct creamy consistency.

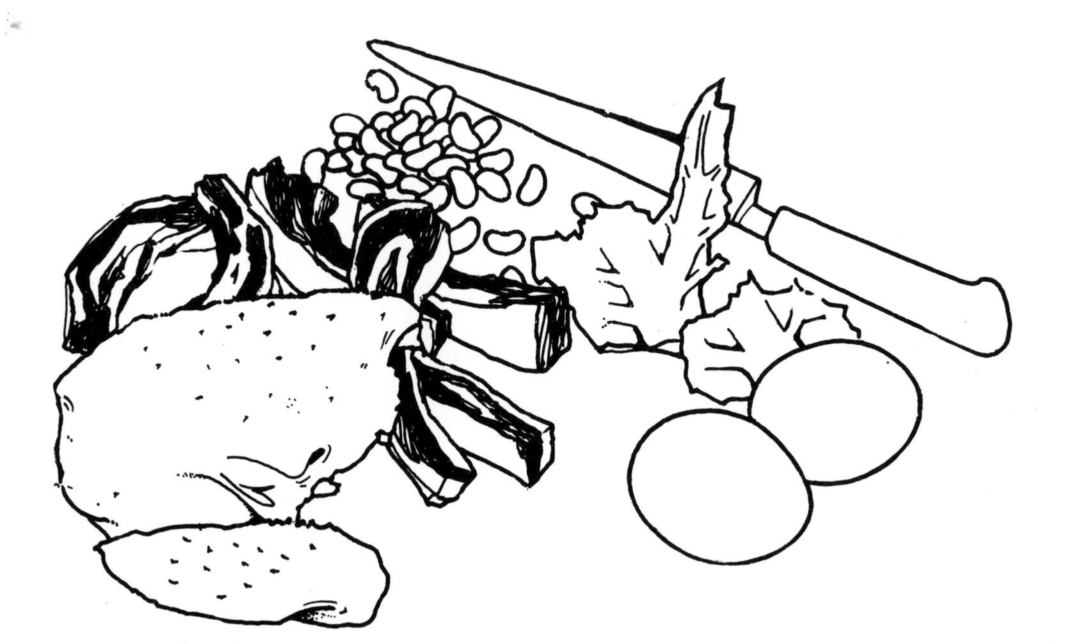

Baked Yogurt-topped Chicken

METRIC/IMPERIAL
15 g/½ oz butter
2 tablespoons finely chopped onion
2 sticks celery, finely chopped
50 g/2 oz button mushrooms, sliced
175 g/6 oz cooked chicken, finely chopped
50 g/2 oz cooked ham, finely chopped
1 tablespoon freshly chopped parsley
Topping:
1 × 150 g/5 oz carton natural yogurt
2 egg yolks
squeeze of lemon juice

AMERICAN
1 tablespoon butter
2 tablespoons finely chopped onion
2 stalks celery, finely chopped
½ cup sliced button mushrooms
¾ cup finely chopped cooked chicken
¼ cup finely chopped cooked ham
1 tablespoon freshly chopped parsley
Topping:
1 × 5 oz carton unflavored yogurt
2 egg yolks
squeeze of lemon juice

Heat the butter in a pan and add the onion, celery and mushrooms. Cover and cook gently for 10 minutes. Add the chicken, ham and parsley. Turn into a 900 ml/1½ pint/4 cup ovenproof dish and press down well.

Beat together the yogurt and egg yolks, then stir in the lemon juice. Spoon over the top of the chicken mixture. Place in a preheated moderately hot oven (190°C/375°F, Gas Mark 5) and cook for 20 minutes until the topping is set. Serve warm with savoury rice.

Serves 1 adult and 1 child
For children over 1 year old

Chicken Casserole

METRIC/IMPERIAL
2 small chicken joints
1 1/2 teaspoons plain flour
250 ml/8 fl oz chicken stock or apple juice
1 tablespoon tomato purée
1 bay leaf
sprig of parsley
1 small onion, finely chopped

AMERICAN
2 small chicken joints
1 1/2 teaspoons all-purpose flour
1 cup chicken stock or apple juice
1 tablespoon tomato paste
1 bay leaf
sprig of parsley
1 small onion, finely chopped

Wipe the chicken joints and place in a small casserole. Blend the flour with a little of the stock or apple juice in a bowl. Stir in the remaining stock, and the tomato purée (paste). Pour over the chicken joints. Add the bay leaf, sprig of parsley, and onion. Cover the casserole. Place in a preheated moderate oven (180°C/350°F, Gas Mark 4) for 45 minutes or until the chicken is tender.

Lift out the chicken joints and place on a serving dish. Strain the sauce through a sieve (strainer) and pour over the chicken joints. Serve with jacket baked potatoes and Brussels sprouts, or vegetables of your choice.

For babies aged 6 months to 1 year: purée a little chicken flesh with 1 tablespoon of potato scooped away from the skin and sufficient of the cooking liquid to give the right creamy consistency.

For children aged 1 to 2 years: remove the chicken from the bones and cut into small pieces. Serve with chopped vegetables.

Serves 1 adult and 1 child

CHICKEN CASSEROLE
(Photograph: British Poultry Meat Association)

Chicken and Rice Moulds

METRIC/IMPERIAL
2 small chicken quarters, skinned
300 ml/½ pint chicken stock
75 g/3 oz long-grain rice
1 small red pepper, seeded and chopped
4 eggs
150 ml/¼ pint single cream
2 tablespoons freshly chopped parsley

AMERICAN
2 small chicken quarters, skinned
1¼ cups chicken stock
½ cup long-grain rice
1 small red pepper, seeded and chopped
4 eggs
⅔ cup light cream
2 tablespoons freshly chopped parsley

Divide each chicken quarter into two pieces. Put the stock and chicken into the base of a pressure cooker, and lay the trivet on top. Line a separator with foil (or use a solid one), then add the rice and chopped pepper with 300 ml/½ pint/1¼ cups water. Wrap two of the eggs in foil and stand these in the separator with the rice, pepper and water. Stand the separator on top of the trivet. Close the cooker and bring to 'H' pressure. Cook for 5 minutes and reduce the pressure slowly.

Lift out the eggs, remove the foil and cool the eggs in cold water. Rinse the rice and pepper with hot water, then transfer to a mixing bowl. Cool the chicken and remove the meat from the bones; chop into small pieces and add to the rice. Chop the hard-boiled eggs and add these to the mixture. Beat together the cream and the remaining two eggs and stir into the chicken mixture with the parsley.

Transfer the mixture to six greased teacups or steaming moulds. (At this stage, salt and pepper can be added to the adult portions.) Cover the teacups or moulds with foil.

Pour 600 ml/1 pint/2 cups water into the cooker. Stand three moulds on the base, cover with the trivet and stand three more on top. Close the cooker, bring to 'H' pressure and cook for 5 minutes. Reduce the pressure slowly.

Serve with a green salad.

For children over 1 year old

Chicken Fricassée

METRIC/IMPERIAL
25 g/1 oz butter or margarine
25 g/1 oz plain flour
250 ml/8 fl oz milk
1 tablespoon lemon juice
225 g/8 oz cooked chicken, chopped
1 × 100 g/4 oz packet frozen sweetcorn kernels, thawed
225 g/8 oz creamed potatoes
1 tablespoon boiled carrot slices to garnish

AMERICAN
2 tablespoons butter or margarine
1/4 cup all-purpose flour
1 cup milk
1 tablespoon lemon juice
1 cup chopped cooked chicken
1 × 1/4 lb package frozen sweetcorn kernels, thawed
1 cup creamed potatoes
1 tablespoon boiled carrot slices to garnish

Melt the butter or margarine in a saucepan, add the flour and mix well. Add the milk gradually, stirring constantly, and simmer gently for 5 minutes. Stir in the lemon juice. Add the chicken and sweetcorn and reheat slowly until thoroughly heated through.

Serve the chicken sauce in a hot dish and pipe or spoon a border of creamed potato around it. Garnish with slices of boiled carrot. Serve with a green vegetable.

For babies aged 6 months to 1 year: purée a little of the chicken mixture, adding sufficient sauce to make the right creamy consistency.

FISH

Baker's Soufflé

METRIC/IMPERIAL
75 g/3 oz butter, softened
8 slices French bread, 5 mm/¼ inch thick
100 g/4 oz smoked haddock
approximately 150 ml/¼ pint milk
25 g/1 oz plain flour
3 eggs, separated
50 g/2 oz Cheddar cheese, grated

AMERICAN
¼ cup plus 2 tablespoons butter, softened
8 slices French bread, ¼ inch thick
¼ lb smoked haddock
approximately ⅔ cup milk
¼ cup all-purpose flour
3 eggs, separated
½ cup grated Cheddar cheese

Thickly butter the inside of a 900 ml/1½ pint/4 cup soufflé dish. Spread 50 g/2 oz/¼ cup of the softened butter on both sides of the bread slices and use to line the sides of the soufflé dish. Poach the haddock in milk for 5 minutes, then strain, reserving the milk. Make up the milk to 150 ml/¼ pint/⅔ cup, if necessary. Flake the haddock, taking care to remove all bones. Whisk the remaining butter, the flour and the poaching milk together in a pan. Bring to the boil, whisking continuously. When the sauce has thickened, cool slightly, then beat in the egg yolks. Add the haddock and cheese. Whisk the egg whites until just stiff and fold into the sauce mixture. Pour into the soufflé dish being careful not to disturb the bread. Bake in a preheated moderately hot oven (200°C/400°F, Gas Mark 6) for about 35 minutes, until well risen and golden brown. Serve immediately with peas or French (green) beans.
For babies aged 6 months to 1 year: scoop some of the moist soufflé from the centre. Add a little boiled milk, if necessary, to make a creamy consistency. Serve with puréed vegetables.
Serves 1 adult and 2 children

FISH WITH YOGURT SAUCE *(page 50)*
(Photograph: White Fish Authority)

Fish with Yogurt Sauce

METRIC/IMPERIAL
750 g/1 1/2 lb white fish fillets, skinned
100 g/4 oz mushrooms, sliced
1 tablespoon lemon juice
5 tablespoons natural yogurt
lemon slices to garnish

AMERICAN
1 1/2 lb white fish fillets, skinned
1 cup sliced mushrooms
1 tablespoon lemon juice
1/3 cup unflavored yogurt
lemon slices to garnish

Lightly butter the centre of a piece of aluminium foil about 20 × 40 cm/ 8 × 16 inches. Cut the fish into 2 adult and 2 children's portions and lay these on the foil. Cover the fish with sliced mushrooms and sprinkle with lemon juice. Fold the foil to make a parcel and bake in a preheated moderately hot oven (190°C/375°F, Gas Mark 5) for 30 minutes. Open one corner of the foil and pour the juices into a saucepan. Add the yogurt and reheat but do not boil. Serve with savoury rice and garnish with lemon slices.
For babies aged 6 months to 1 year: purée a little fish and savoury rice with the sauce. (Make sure there are no bones in the fish.)
Note: If preferred, the adults' fish can be well-seasoned and cooked in a separate foil parcel. Separate sauces will have to be made.

Fish Puffs

METRIC/IMPERIAL
50 g/2 oz plain flour
2 teaspoons cooking oil
5 tablespoons lukewarm water
100 g/4 oz cooked white fish, flaked
2 teaspoons lemon juice
1 tablespoon freshly chopped parsley
1 egg white
oil for deep frying

AMERICAN
1/2 cup all-purpose flour
2 teaspoons cooking oil
1/3 cup lukewarm water
1/4 lb cooked white fish, flaked
2 teaspoons lemon juice
1 tablespoon freshly chopped parsley
1 egg white
oil for deep frying

Sift the flour into a bowl. Mix to a thick batter with the oil and water. Stir in the fish (making sure there are no bones), lemon juice and parsley. Whisk the egg white until stiff. Fold gently into the fish using a metal spoon.

Deep fry spoonfuls of the mixture in oil heated to 190°C/375°F, until the puffs are golden brown and crisp. Lift out with a slotted spoon and drain on absorbent kitchen paper. Serve hot with creamy mashed potatoes and peas.
Serves 1 adult and 1 child
For children over 1 year old

Vegetable and Fish Pie

METRIC/IMPERIAL
500 g/1 lb white fish fillets, skinned
300 ml/½ pint milk
25 g/1 oz butter
2 tablespoons cornflour
little extra milk
1 teaspoon tomato purée
50 g/2 oz carrots, cooked and diced
50 g/2 oz peas, cooked
225 g/8 oz potatoes, cooked and mashed
50 g/2 oz swede, cooked and mashed
2 tablespoons creamy milk or single cream

AMERICAN
1 lb white fish fillets, skinned
1¼ cups milk
2 tablespoons butter
2 tablespoons cornstarch
little extra milk
1 teaspoon tomato paste
¼ cup diced carrots, cooked
¼ cup peas, cooked
1 cup mashed potatoes
¼ cup mashed rutabaga
2 tablespoons half-and-half or light cream

Place the fish in an ovenproof dish. Pour in the milk and dot the fish with butter. Bake in a preheated moderate oven (180°C/350°F, Gas Mark 4) for 20 minutes. Drain and reserve the cooking liquid. Flake the fish, taking care to check that all bones have been removed. Blend the cornflour (cornstarch) with a little extra milk. Stir into the reserved cooking liquid in a saucepan and place over a moderate heat, stirring continuously until the sauce thickens. Add the tomato purée (paste).

Combine the fish, carrots, peas and sauce in the ovenproof dish. Mix the potato and swede (rutabaga) together thoroughly, adding a little milk or single (light) cream to make a creamy mixture. Spread this on top of the fish and the other vegetables and return to a hot oven (220°C/425°F, Gas Mark 7) to reheat and brown the top.

For babies aged 6 months to 1 year: purée a little of the fish and vegetables in the sauce below the potato topping.

Fish Chowder

METRIC/IMPERIAL

100 g/4 oz white fish fillet
150 ml/¼ pint milk
120 ml/4 fl oz water
100 g/4 oz potato, cubed
1 carrot, thinly sliced
1 small onion, finely chopped
1 tablespoon cooking oil
3 tablespoons cream
25 g/1 oz peeled shrimps
1 teaspoon freshly chopped parsley

AMERICAN

¼ lb white fish fillet
⅔ cup milk
½ cup water
⅔ cup diced potato
1 carrot, thinly sliced
1 small onion, finely chopped
1 tablespoon cooking oil
3 tablespoons cream
2 tablespoons shelled shrimp
1 teaspoon freshly chopped parsley

Wash the fish and poach gently in the milk and water for about 10 minutes. Remove the fish, discard the skin and flake the flesh, checking that all bones have been removed. Cook the potato and carrot in the fish liquor. In a separate pan, fry the onion in oil until golden. Add the onion to the potato and fish liquor in the saucepan. Stir in the cream, flaked fish, shrimps and parsley. Heat gently for 5 minutes, but do not boil.
For babies aged 6 months to 1 year: select small pieces of fish, carrot and a little potato, and purée with some of the liquid.
Serves 1 adult and 1 child

Fish with Parsley Sauce

METRIC/IMPERIAL

500 g/1 lb white fish fillets, skinned
1 tablespoon freshly chopped parsley
1 teaspoon mild cream of horseradish sauce
300 ml/½ pint milk
25 g/1 oz margarine
25 g/1 oz cornflour
1 egg, hard-boiled and chopped

AMERICAN

1 lb white fish fillets, skinned
1 tablespoon freshly chopped parsley
1 teaspoon mild cream of horseradish sauce
1¼ cups milk
2 tablespoons margarine
¼ cup cornstarch
1 egg, hard-boiled and chopped

Cut the fish into suitable serving portions and put in a shallow pan. Sprinkle with the parsley, add the horseradish and pour the milk over. Dot with margarine. Cover the pan and poach the fish for 10 to 15 minutes. Blend the cornflour (cornstarch) with a little extra milk, then add to the milk in the pan, stirring and tilting the pan as the sauce thickens. Finally, stir in the egg. Serve with diced carrots or peas.
For babies aged 6 months to 1 year: purée a little fish with the sauce. (Make sure there are no bones in the fish.) Purée a small portion of carrots or peas separately.

FISH CHOWDER
(Photograph: White Fish Authority)

EGGS

Bubblyata

METRIC/IMPERIAL
3 tomatoes, skinned and roughly chopped
25 g/1 oz butter
6 eggs
2 tablespoons cooked peas
2 teaspoons chopped chives
1 tablespoon cream or top-of-the-milk
fingers of buttered toast to serve

AMERICAN
3 tomatoes, skinned and roughly chopped
2 tablespoons butter
6 eggs
2 tablespoons cooked peas
2 teaspoons chopped chives
1 tablespoon cream or half-and-half
fingers of buttered toast to serve

Cook the tomatoes in butter for 2 to 3 minutes. Lightly beat the eggs, and stir in the cooked peas and chives. Pour on to the tomatoes and scramble the eggs in the usual way, adding the cream just before the eggs set. Serve with fingers of toast.
For children over 1 year old

Farmhouse Scramble

METRIC/IMPERIAL
1 medium onion, finely chopped
50 g/2 oz butter
500 g/1 lb green cabbage, shredded
4 tablespoons beef stock
6 eggs
1 teaspoon freshly chopped parsley

AMERICAN
1 medium onion, finely chopped
1/4 cup butter
6 cups shredded green cabbage
1/4 cup beef stock
6 eggs
1 teaspoon freshly chopped parsley

Using a large pan with a well fitting lid, cook the onion in 25 g/1 oz/2 tablespoons butter for 5 minutes, but do not allow them to brown. Add the cabbage and the stock. With the lid on the pan, cook over a low heat, shaking the pan at intervals, until the cabbage is beginning to soften, about 15 minutes. Transfer the cabbage to a serving dish and keep warm. In a clean pan, melt the remaining butter and scramble the eggs, adding the parsley just as the eggs are starting to set. Pile the eggs on top of the cabbage and serve immediately.
For children over 1 year old

Haddock Scramble

METRIC/IMPERIAL	AMERICAN
225 g/8 oz smoked haddock, cooked	*½ lb smoked haddock, cooked*
25 g/1 oz butter	*2 tablespoons butter*
6 eggs	*6 eggs*
½ teaspoon grated lemon rind	*½ teaspoon grated lemon rind*
2 teaspoons freshly chopped parsley	*2 teaspoons freshly chopped parsley*
1 tablespoon cream or top-of-the-milk	*1 tablespoon cream or half-and-half*

Flake the haddock carefully, making sure that all bones have been removed. Melt the butter in a saucepan, add the haddock and cook slowly until heated through. Beat the eggs lightly; add the grated lemon rind and chopped parsley. Pour on to the haddock and scramble the eggs as usual, adding cream just before the eggs set.
For babies aged 6 months to 1 year: remove baby's portion of scrambled egg while it is very moist. Purée a little fish with 2 tablespoons of boiled milk. Mix with the egg.

Egg and Cheese Croquettes

METRIC/IMPERIAL	AMERICAN
3 eggs, hard-boiled and shelled	*3 eggs, hard-boiled and shelled*
225 g/8 oz mashed potato	*1 cup mashed potato*
2 spring onions, chopped, or 1 tablespoon finely chopped onion	*2 scallions, chopped, or 1 tablespoon finely chopped onion*
50 g/2 oz Cheddar cheese, grated	*½ cup grated Cheddar cheese*
1 egg, beaten	*1 egg, beaten*
2-4 tablespoons browned breadcrumbs	*2-4 tablespoons browned breadcrumbs*
oil for deep frying	*oil for deep frying*

Chop the hard-boiled eggs and add to the mashed potato with the chopped onion and grated cheese. Mix well. Reserve 1 tablespoon of the beaten egg and mix the remainder into the potato mixture to bind. Roll into 8 croquette shapes using a floured board or floured hands. Brush each croquette with beaten egg and coat with the browned breadcrumbs. Deep fry in oil at a temperature of 190°C/375°F, until golden brown in colour. Drain on absorbent kitchen paper. Serve with tomatoes.
For children over 1 year old

Eggs Florentine

METRIC/IMPERIAL
2 eggs
100 g/4 oz cooked spinach purée
pat of butter
pinch of grated nutmeg
Sauce:
25 g/1 oz butter or margarine
25 g/1 oz plain flour
250 ml/8 fl oz milk
50 g/2 oz Double Gloucester cheese, grated

AMERICAN
2 eggs
2/3 cup cooked spinach purée
pat of butter
pinch of grated nutmeg
Sauce:
2 tablespoons butter or margarine
1/4 cup all-purpose flour
1 cup milk
1/2 cup grated Cheddar cheese

Boil the eggs for only 7 minutes so that they are not completely hard. Cool under running cold water. Peel off the shells carefully. Mix the spinach purée with the butter and the grated nutmeg. Place in the bottom of a small ovenproof dish. Cut the eggs in half lengthwise and arrange on the spinach, cut-side down.

Put the butter or margarine, flour and milk in a saucepan. Bring to the boil, whisking continuously. Cook for 2 to 3 minutes. Stir in three-quarters of the cheese. Pour the sauce over the eggs and the spinach. Sprinkle the remaining grated cheese over the top. Brown under a moderate grill (broiler). Serve with sliced tomatoes.
Serves 1 adult and 1 child
For children over 1 year old

Egg Nests

METRIC/IMPERIAL
2 beefburgers
225 g/8 oz creamed potato
2 eggs

AMERICAN
2 beefburgers
1 cup creamed potato
2 eggs

Thaw the beefburgers first, if frozen. Place the beefburgers on an ovenproof plate. Either pipe 2 layers of potato around the edge of each beefburger using a fluted nozzle and a piping bag, or spoon the potato around the edge of each beefburger to form a nest shape. Break the eggs individually into a cup and tip one into each of the 'nests'. Bake on the centre shelf of a moderately hot oven (200°C/400°F, Gas Mark 6) until the potato is golden and the egg is just set, about 20 minutes.
Serves 1 adult and 1 child
For children over 1 year old

EGGS FLORENTINE
(Photograph: The Tupperware Company)

CHEESE

Gnocchi

METRIC/IMPERIAL	AMERICAN
600 ml/1 pint milk	*2½ cups milk*
½ teaspoon made mustard	*½ teaspoon made mustard*
175 g/6 oz fine semolina	*1 cup fine semolina*
50 g/2 oz Cheddar cheese, grated	*½ cup grated Cheddar cheese*
1 egg, beaten	*1 egg, beaten*
25 g/1 oz Parmesan cheese, grated	*¼ cup grated Parmesan cheese*

Bring the milk to the boil in a saucepan. Add the mustard, then tip in the semolina and cook, stirring, until the mixture thickens and leaves the sides of the pan – it will only take a few minutes. Remove from the heat. Blend in the grated Cheddar cheese and the beaten egg.

Turn into a greased shallow baking tin about 23 × 23 cm/9 × 9 inches. Smooth out evenly and leave until cold. Mark into squares and sprinkle with Parmesan cheese. Bake in a preheated moderately hot oven (190°C/375°F, Gas Mark 5) for 25 minutes. Serve with grilled (broiled) tomatoes and peas.

For children over 1 year old

Potato Lorraine

METRIC/IMPERIAL	AMERICAN
500 g/1 lb potatoes, boiled	*1 lb potatoes, boiled*
100 g/4 oz Cheddar cheese, grated	*1 cup grated Cheddar cheese*
2 large eggs (grade 1 or 2)	*2 large eggs*
150 ml/¼ pint milk	*⅔ cup milk*
pinch of grated nutmeg	*pinch of grated nutmeg*
25 g/1 oz butter	*2 tablespoons butter*

Slice the potatoes. Sprinkle the bottom of a greased pie dish with half the cheese. Cover evenly with the potatoes. Beat the eggs, milk and nutmeg together. Pour over the potatoes, cover with the remaining cheese and dot with the butter. Bake in a preheated moderately hot oven (190°C/375°F, Gas Mark 5) for 30 minutes until the custard is set and browned. Serve hot with a lightly cooked green vegetable, or cold with a green salad.

For babies aged 6 months to 1 year: purée a little of the pie, mixing to a creamy consistency with a tablespoon of boiled milk if required.

Cheese and Cauliflower Soufflé

METRIC/IMPERIAL	AMERICAN
100 g/4 oz cauliflower, divided into florets	*¼ lb cauliflower, divided into florets*
25 g/1 oz butter or margarine	*2 tablespoons butter or margarine*
1½ tablespoons plain flour	*1½ tablespoons all-purpose flour*
120 ml/4 fl oz milk	*½ cup milk*
2 eggs, separated	*2 eggs, separated*
50 g/2 oz Cheddar cheese, grated	*½ cup grated Cheddar cheese*

Cook the cauliflower florets in boiling water for about 10 minutes or until tender. Drain and cool slightly.

Melt the butter or margarine in a small saucepan, add the flour and cook over a gentle heat for one minute, stirring continuously. Stir in the milk all at once and cook, stirring, until thickened and smooth.

Place the cauliflower in a blender goblet with the egg yolks and purée until smooth. Alternatively, mash the cauliflower to a purée with a fork and mix in the egg yolks.

Reserve a little of the grated cheese for the top of the soufflé. Stir the remainder into the white sauce mixture with the cauliflower purée, until thoroughly blended.

Whisk the egg whites until stiff but not dry and fold into the cauliflower mixture. Spoon into a lightly greased 600 ml/1 pint/2½ cup soufflé dish. Sprinkle with the reserved cheese. Stand the dish on a baking sheet and bake in a preheated moderately hot oven (190°C/375°F, Gas Mark 5) for 20 to 25 minutes until golden brown and just set. Serve warm with diced carrot and peas.

For babies aged 6 months to 1 year: mix a small portion taken from the centre of the soufflé with a little boiled milk. Serve with 1 tablespoon of the vegetables, puréed in a blender.

Serves 1 adult and 1 child

Seaside Pasta

METRIC/IMPERIAL
100 g/4 oz pasta shells
25 g/1 oz butter or margarine
25 g/1 oz plain flour
450 ml/¾ pint milk
100 g/4 oz Edam cheese, grated
pinch of mixed herbs
1 × 100 g/4 oz can tuna fish, drained and flaked
1 tomato, sliced, to garnish

AMERICAN
1 cup pasta shells
2 tablespoons butter or margarine
¼ cup all-purpose flour
2 cups milk
1 cup grated Edam cheese cheddar
~~*pinch of mixed herbs*~~ mustard
1 × 4 oz can tuna fish, drained and flaked 1 7½ oz can
1 tomato, sliced, to garnish

Cook the pasta according to the directions on the packet, then drain thoroughly. Place the butter or margarine, flour and milk in a saucepan. Heat, whisking continuously, until the sauce thickens. Add half of the grated cheese, and the mixed herbs.

Place the pasta in a lightly greased 1 litre/2 pint/5 cup ovenproof dish. Mix in the flaked tuna fish and pour over the sauce. Sprinkle the remaining grated cheese over the top. Garnish with the sliced tomato. Place in a preheated moderately hot oven (200°C/400°F, Gas Mark 6) and cook for 20 minutes. Serve with a green salad.

For babies aged 6 months to 1 year: purée a little of the pasta, tuna fish, cheese sauce and skinned tomato.

If freezing cook noodles 4-5 min then ∅ mushy

Cheese Pudding

METRIC/IMPERIAL
300 ml/½ pint milk
50 g/2 oz white breadcrumbs
1 large egg, beaten
50 g/2 oz mild Cheddar cheese, grated

AMERICAN
1¼ cups milk
1 cup white breadcrumbs
1 large egg, beaten
½ cup grated mild Cheddar cheese

Bring the milk to the boil in a saucepan, stir in the breadcrumbs and leave to soak for 20 minutes. Add the beaten egg and the cheese and mix well. Pour into a greased 600 ml/1 pint/2½ cup ovenproof dish and bake in a preheated moderately hot oven (190°C/375°F, Gas Mark 5) for about 25 minutes or until well risen and golden brown. Serve with mixed diced vegetables.

For babies aged 6 months to 1 year: mash with a little extra boiled milk to a creamy consistency.

Serves 1 adult and 2 children

SEASIDE PASTA
(Photograph: Dutch Dairy Bureau)

Stuffed Marrow (Squash)

METRIC/IMPERIAL	AMERICAN
1 young marrow	*1 young summer squash*
3 tomatoes, skinned	*3 tomatoes, skinned*
100 g/4 oz cooked rice	*2/3 cup cooked rice*
100 g/4 oz Cheddar cheese, diced	*1 cup diced Cheddar cheese*
75 g/3 oz cooked ham, chopped	*1/2 cup chopped cooked ham*
1 tablespoon freshly chopped parsley	*1 tablespoon freshly chopped parsley*
25 g/1 oz butter, melted	*2 tablespoons butter, melted*

Wipe the marrow (squash) and cut into slices 4 cm/1 1/2 inches thick and remove the seeds. Roughly chop the tomatoes and mix with the rice, cheese, ham and parsley. Lay the marrow rings in a well-buttered ovenproof dish and fill with the stuffing. Brush the marrow (squash) with melted butter. Cover the dish with kitchen foil and bake in preheated moderate oven (180°C/350°F, Gas Mark 4) for about 25 minutes, or until the marrow (squash) is tender. Serve with creamed spinach.

For children over 1 year old

Note: The same stuffing can be used for tomatoes, aubergines (eggplant) and other suitable vegetables.

SALADS

Pasta Salad

METRIC/IMPERIAL	AMERICAN
50 g/2 oz cooked small pasta shapes	*1/4 cup cooked small pasta shapes*
50 g/2 oz cooked green peas	*1/4 cup cooked green peas*
2 sticks celery, chopped	*2 stalks celery, chopped*
50 g/2 oz lean ham, chopped	*1/4 cup chopped lean cooked ham*
50 g/2 oz corned beef, diced	*1/4 cup diced corned beef*
Dressing:	**Dressing:**
1 tablespoon lemon juice	*1 tablespoon lemon juice*
1 tablespoon salad oil	*1 tablespoon salad oil*

Mix all the salad ingredients together. Blend the lemon juice and oil and pour over the salad. Toss lightly to mix.

Serves 1 adult and 1 child over 1 year old

Florida Salad

METRIC/IMPERIAL
2 large oranges
2 dessert apples, peeled and grated
1 tablespoon lemon juice
100 g/4 oz cottage cheese
1 × 150 g/5 oz carton natural yogurt
1 stick celery, finely chopped
pinch of ground cinnamon
sprigs of mint to garnish
To serve:
lettuce
brown bread and butter

AMERICAN
2 large oranges
2 dessert apples, peeled and grated
1 tablespoon lemon juice
½ cup low fat cream cheese
1 × 5 oz carton unflavored yogurt
1 stalk celery, finely chopped
pinch of ground cinnamon
sprigs of mint to garnish
To serve:
lettuce
brown bread and butter

Cut the oranges in half and scoop out the centres with a sharp knife, reserving the fruit and juice. Remove the skin and any pith from the orange flesh. Sprinkle the apple with lemon juice. Mix the orange, apple, cheese, yogurt, celery and cinnamon together. Divide the mixture between the orange cups. Decorate each one with a sprig of mint. Serve on a bed of lettuce with brown bread and butter.
For babies aged 6 months to 1 year: sieve (strain) 1 tablespoon of cottage cheese (low fat cream cheese). Add 1 teaspoon fresh orange juice and sufficient natural (unflavored) yogurt to give a creamy consistency.

Fruity Salad

METRIC/IMPERIAL
225 g/8 oz white cabbage, finely shredded
3 small oranges
50 g/2 oz dates, stoned and chopped
175 g/6 oz Leicester cheese, diced
Dressing:
2 tablespoons orange juice (reserved from oranges)
2 tablespoons salad oil
To serve:
lettuce
brown bread and butter

AMERICAN
3 cups shredded white cabbage
3 small oranges
1/4 cup chopped pitted dates
1 cup diced Cheddar cheese
Dressing:
2 tablespoons orange juice (reserved from oranges)
2 tablespoons salad oil
To serve:
lettuce
brown bread and butter

Put the cabbage into a salad bowl. Remove the peel and pith from the oranges, cutting spirally around the fruit with a very sharp knife. Cut the oranges into segments between the membranes being careful to retain any juice. Add orange segments to the cabbage, then mix in the dates and cheese. Blend together the orange juice and salad oil. Pour the dressing over the salad and toss lightly. Serve with lettuce and brown bread and butter.
For children over 1 year old

Crunchy Winter Salad

METRIC/IMPERIAL
1 green-skinned dessert apple, thinly sliced
1 red-skinned dessert apple, thinly sliced
2 tablespoons lemon juice
225 g/8 oz red cabbage, finely shredded
4 sticks celery, chopped
50 g/2 oz salted peanuts, chopped
French bread to serve

AMERICAN
1 green-skinned dessert apple, thinly sliced
1 red-skinned dessert apple, thinly sliced
2 tablespoons lemon juice
3 cups finely shredded red cabbage
4 stalks celery, chopped
1/2 cup chopped salted peanuts
French bread to serve

Sprinkle the apple with the lemon juice, then mix all the ingredients together. Toss the salad lightly to distribute the lemon juice. Serve with French bread and butter.
For children over 2 years old
For children aged 1 to 2 years: grate the peeled apple and combine with finely shredded cabbage.

SPEEDY CHICKEN PIE *(page 42)*
(Photograph: Flour Advisory Bureau)

New Vegetable Salad

METRIC/IMPERIAL

500 g/1 lb small new potatoes
100 g/4 oz cauliflower, broken into florets
3 carrots, cut into tiny dice
4 sticks celery, cut into tiny dice
100 g/4 oz French beans, cut into 2 cm/½ inch pieces
100 g/4 oz shelled peas
1 × 150 g/5 oz carton natural yogurt
1 tablespoon freshly chopped parsley to garnish
lettuce to serve

AMERICAN

1 lb small new potatoes
1 cup cauliflower florets
3 carrots, cut into tiny dice
4 stalks celery, cut into tiny dice
½ cup diced green beans
¾ cup shelled peas
1 × 5 oz carton unflavored yogurt
1 tablespoon freshly chopped parsley to garnish
lettuce to serve

Boil the potatoes until just cooked. In a separate pan, cook the cauliflower, carrots, celery, beans and peas for 2 to 3 minutes only. Coat the vegetables with yogurt while they are still warm. When cool, chill in the refrigerator. Sprinkle with chopped parsley. Serve with lettuce.

For babies aged 6 months to 1 year: purée a little of each cooked vegetable and mix to a creamy consistency with yogurt.

DESSERTS

Raspberry Cream Crunch

METRIC/IMPERIAL
25 g/1 oz butter
6 digestive biscuits, crushed
50 g/2 oz sugar
50 g/2 oz wholewheat semolina
450 ml/¾ pint milk
1 × 150 g/5 oz carton raspberry yogurt
50 g/2 oz cream cheese
50 g/2 oz fresh raspberries to decorate

AMERICAN
2 tablespoons butter
6 Graham crackers, crushed
¼ cup sugar
⅓ cup wholewheat semolina
2 cups milk
1 × 5 oz carton raspberry yogurt
¼ cup cream cheese
½ cup fresh raspberries to decorate

Melt the butter in a saucepan and add the crushed biscuits (crackers). Mix well and allow to cool. In a saucepan, mix the sugar, semolina and milk. Bring to the boil, stirring continuously, and simmer for 2 to 3 minutes. Cool slightly, then beat in the yogurt and cream cheese. Pour the mixture into individual dishes and top each with a little of the crumb mixture. Place in the refrigerator to set. Decorate with fresh raspberries just before serving.
For babies aged 6 months to 1 year: serve without the crumb topping.

Summer Pudding

METRIC/IMPERIAL	AMERICAN
6-8 slices of soft white bread, crusts removed	*6-8 slices of soft white bread, crusts removed*
1 kg/2 lb mixed summer fruit, such as gooseberries, black and red currants, raspberries and strawberries	*6 cups mixed summer fruit, such as gooseberries, black and red currants, raspberries and strawberries*
150 g/5 oz caster sugar, or to taste	*2/3 cup sugar, or to taste*

Arrange the bread slices to make a complete lining around the sides and bottom of a 1 litre/2 pint/5 cup pudding basin (slope-sided mold) or soufflé dish, cutting and shaping if necessary and reserving some for the top. Lightly stew those fruits normally eaten cooked (such as gooseberries, black and red currants) with a little water. Sweeten to taste. Allow the stewed fruit to cool; strain and reserve the juice. Mix the stewed fruit with the uncooked fruit and sugar.

Moisten the bread lining with the reserved juice and transfer the fruit mixture to the bowl. Top with the remaining slices of bread, pressing the fruit filling down firmly. Cover the bowl with a plate or saucer which just fits inside the rim. Place a heavy weight on the plate to compress the fruit. Leave overnight in the refrigerator. To serve, turn out into a serving dish. Pour any remaining juice over the pudding. Serve with cream, or ice cream, if liked.

For babies aged 6 months to 1 year: purée fruits selected from the inside of the pudding.

Baked Apple Surprise

METRIC/IMPERIAL
4 cooking apples, cored
50 g/2 oz stoned dates
25 g/1 oz butter
4 tablespoons golden syrup
4 teaspoons cottage cheese

AMERICAN
4 baking apples, cored
1/4 cup pitted dates
2 tablespoons butter
1/4 cup light corn syrup
4 teaspoons low fat cream cheese

Score the skin of the apples around the middle. Place them in an ovenproof dish. Fill the core cavities with the dates and top with butter. Spoon the syrup over the apples and bake them in a moderately hot oven (190°C/375°F, Gas Mark 5) for about 40 minutes, or until the apples are tender. Top each apple with a small spoonful of cottage cheese (low fat cream cheese).
For babies aged 6 months to 1 year: sieve (strain) a small portion of the apple pulp only. Sweeten with a little syrup.

Apple Snow

METRIC/IMPERIAL
500 g/1 lb cooking apples, peeled, cored and sliced
75 g/3 oz caster sugar
2 tablespoons water
2 teaspoons grated orange rind
2 egg whites
1 small orange, outer skin and pith removed

AMERICAN
4 cups diced baking apples
1/3 cup sugar
2 tablespoons water
2 teaspoons grated zest of orange
2 egg whites
1 small orange, outer skin and pith removed

Place the apples, sugar and water in a saucepan. Cover, and cook gently until the apples are soft. Press the apple mixture through a sieve (strainer) and add the grated orange rind. When cool, beat the egg whites until stiff and fold into the apple purée. Chill in the refrigerator. Garnish with thin slices of orange before serving.
For babies aged 6 months to 1 year: serve apple snow without the orange flesh.
For children over 1 year old: remove all skin from the orange slices and serve flesh only.

Apricot Cream

METRIC/IMPERIAL	AMERICAN
225 g/8 oz dried apricots	*1¼ cups dried apricots*
1 large can evaporated milk	*1 large can evaporated milk*
2 tablespoons orange juice	*2 tablespoons orange juice*
50 g/2 oz icing sugar, sifted	*½ cup confectioners' sugar, sifted*
few grapes, peeled, halved and seeded, to decorate	*few grapes peeled, halved and pitted, to decorate*

Cover the apricots with boiling water and leave to soak overnight. Leave the can of milk in the refrigerator overnight to chill thoroughly.

The next day, place the apricots and water in a saucepan and simmer until tender. Drain the fruit and rub through a nylon sieve (strainer) or purée in a blender. Beat the evaporated milk in a bowl, and when it is starting to thicken add the orange juice. Stir in the apricot purée and sugar. Pour into a serving dish and chill in the refrigerator before serving. Arrange the grapes on top of the chilled dessert.

For babies aged 6 months to 1 year: serve without the grapes.

Quick Fruit Charlotte

METRIC/IMPERIAL	AMERICAN
50 g/2 oz butter or margarine	*¼ cup butter or margarine*
1 large cooking apple, peeled, cored and thinly sliced	*1 large baking apple, peeled, cored and thinly sliced*
2 thick slices of white sandwich loaf	*2 thick slices white bread*
25 g/1 oz soft brown sugar	*2 tablespoons light brown sugar*

Melt half the butter or margarine in a frying pan (skillet), add the apple slices and cook them gently for about 8 minutes, stirring occasionally, until the apple is just cooked. Meanwhile, remove the crusts from the bread, if wished. Cut the bread into 1 cm/½ inch squares. When the apple is cooked, push to one side of the pan, and add the remaining butter. Add the bread and fry gently for 3 to 4 minutes until crisp on both sides. Mix the apple and bread together and then stir in sugar. Serve at once.

For babies aged 6 months to 1 year: serve the fruit alone, stewed with a little sugar and puréed in a blender.

Serves 1 adult and 1 child

Variations:

In place of the apple, use pear, plums with stones (pits) removed, peaches or banana. If using banana, cook for 2 minutes only.

Orange Princess Pudding

METRIC/IMPERIAL	AMERICAN
1 teaspoon grated orange rind	*1 teaspoon grated zest of orange*
25 g/1 oz margarine	*2 tablespoons margarine*
300 ml/½ pint milk	*1¼ cups milk*
25 g/1 oz sugar	*2 tablespoons sugar*
50 g/2 oz soft breadcrumbs	*1 cup soft breadcrumbs*
2 eggs, separated	*2 eggs, separated*
1 orange, peel and white pith removed, and thinly sliced	*1 orange, peel and white pith removed and thinly sliced*
50 g/2 oz icing sugar, sifted	*½ cup confectioners' sugar, sifted*

Place the orange rind, margarine and milk in a saucepan; cover and heat gently. Remove from the heat, add the sugar and breadcrumbs and cool slightly. Beat the egg yolks into the crumb mixture and pour into a greased ovenproof 600 ml/1 pint/2½ cup serving dish. Bake in a preheated moderate oven (160°C/325°F, Gas Mark 3) for 20 minutes.

Remove from the oven and cover with a layer of orange slices. Whisk the egg whites until very stiff, then fold in the icing (confectioners') sugar. Pile the meringue onto the pudding. Brown quickly in a preheated hot oven (220°C/425°F, Gas Mark 7) for about 10 minutes.

For babies aged 6 months to 1 year: serve a little of the crumb mixture, softened with boiled milk, with some fruit purée.

Danish Red Jelly

METRIC/IMPERIAL	AMERICAN
500 g/1 lb red currants or black currants	*4 cups red currants or black currants*
150 ml/¼ pint water	*⅔ cup water*
50 g/2 oz caster sugar, or to taste	*¼ cup sugar, or to taste*
2 tablespoons cornflour	*2 tablespoons cornstarch*

Place the fruit, water and sugar in a saucepan and stew gently until the fruit is soft. Rub the fruit through a nylon sieve (strainer) and discard pips (seeds) and skin. Mix the cornflour (cornstarch) with a little water and blend into the purée. Return to the heat, stirring continuously as the mixture thickens. Pour into a serving dish and allow to cool. Serve plain, or with yogurt or ice cream.

ORANGE PRINCESS PUDDING

Lunch

Gooseberry Layer Pudding

METRIC/IMPERIAL
50 g/2 oz unsalted butter
100 g/4 oz soft breadcrumbs
25 g/1 oz soft brown sugar
500 g/1 lb fresh or frozen gooseberries
150 ml/¼ pint water
100 g/4 oz caster sugar
2 × 150 g/5 oz cartons apricot yogurt
2 tablespoons grated chocolate to decorate

AMERICAN
¼ cup sweet butter
2 cups soft breadcrumbs
2 tablespoons light brown sugar
1 lb fresh or frozen gooseberries
⅔ cup water
½ cup sugar
2 × 5 oz cartons apricot yogurt
2 tablespoons grated chocolate to decorate

Melt the butter in a saucepan, then remove from the heat. Stir in the breadcrumbs and brown sugar. Leave to cool. Gently stew the gooseberries with the water and sugar. Purée the gooseberries in a blender and allow to cool. Place alternate layers of crumbs, gooseberry purée and yogurt in individual sundae dishes, finishing with a layer of yogurt. Chill in the refrigerator. Before serving, decorate with grated chocolate.
For children over 1 year old

Fruit Fool

METRIC/IMPERIAL
500 g/1 lb fruit, such as gooseberries, rhubarb, black or red currants, blackberries, raspberries
3 tablespoons water
75-175 g/3-6 oz caster sugar
300 ml/½ pint cold custard, prepared according to instructions on packet

AMERICAN
1 lb fruit, such as gooseberries, rhubarb, black or red currants, blackberries, raspberries
3 tablespoons water
½-¾ cup sugar
1¼ cups cold custard, prepared according to instructions on package

Prepare the fruit and place in a saucepan with the water. Bring slowly to the boil, cover, and simmer gently until the fruit is soft. Remove from the heat, and add sugar to taste (different fruits vary in the amount of sweetening they need). Rub through a nylon sieve (strainer) or purée in a blender. Leave until completely cold, then blend the purée with the custard. Transfer to 4 sundae glasses and chill before serving.

Wholegrain Pudding

METRIC/IMPERIAL	AMERICAN
40 g/1½ oz short-grain rice, tapioca, sago or macaroni	*¼ cup short-grain rice, tapioca or sago, or ⅓ cup macaroni*
25 g/1 oz caster sugar	*2 tablespoons sugar*
600 ml/1 pint milk	*2½ cups milk*
25 g/1 oz butter	*2 tablespoons butter*

Place the chosen cereal and sugar in a greased 600 ml/1 pint/2½ cup ovenproof dish. Heat the milk almost to boiling then pour onto the cereal and sugar. Stir well, dot with small pieces of butter and then bake in the bottom of a preheated cool oven (150°C/300°F, Gas Mark 2) for 2 hours.

Crushed Grain Pudding

METRIC/IMPERIAL	AMERICAN
600 ml/1 pint milk	*2½ cups milk*
25 g/1 oz semolina, flaked rice or ground rice	*3 tablespoons semolina flour, flaked rice or ground rice*
25 g/1 oz sugar	*2 tablespoons sugar*

Heat the milk in a saucepan and sprinkle on the grain. Stir until the milk boils and the mixture thickens. Stir in the sugar and continue to cook for a further 4 minutes, stirring constantly. Serve at once.

For a richer flavour, add 25 g/1 oz/2 tablespoons butter and bake in a greased ovenproof dish in the top of a moderately hot oven (200°C/400°F, Gas Mark 6) for 30 minutes.

For babies aged 6 months to 1 year: add a little extra boiled milk and beat to a very smooth consistency. Do not include any dried fruit. Purée a little stewed fruit to serve with the milk pudding, if liked.

Variations:

Before baking, any one of the following may be added to the pudding:

50 g/2 oz/⅓ cup dried fruit

1 teaspoon ground cinnamon, nutmeg or mixed spice

1 teaspoon grated lemon or orange rind

1 beaten egg

4 tablespoons/¼ cup single (light) cream or evaporated milk

For a Chocolate Milk Pudding: blend 2 tablespoons cocoa powder (unsweetened cocoa) with a little of the milk. Mix with the remaining milk and continue as above.

For a Fruit Milk Pudding: place a layer of stewed fruit in the bottom of the dish before the pudding mixture is poured in. Bake as above.

Chocolate and Orange Meringue Pudding

METRIC/IMPERIAL	AMERICAN
600 ml/1 pint milk	*2½ cups milk*
75 g/3 oz plain chocolate, grated	*3 squares semi-sweet chocolate, grated*
50 g/2 oz semolina	*⅓ cup semolina*
grated rind and juice of 1 orange	*grated zest and juice of 1 orange*
2 eggs, separated	*2 eggs, separated*
50 g/2 oz caster sugar	*¼ cup sugar*

Heat the milk in a saucepan, add the chocolate and stir until dissolved. Sprinkle on the semolina and cook slowly, stirring occasionally, for 7 to 10 minutes.

Remove from the heat, stir in the orange juice and half the rind and the egg yolks. Pour into a buttered ovenproof dish.

Whisk the egg whites until stiff, whisk in half the sugar, then fold in the remaining sugar and orange rind, using a metal spoon. Pile on top of the semolina.

Bake in a preheated cool oven (140°C/275°F, Gas Mark 1) until the meringue is brown and crisp.

For babies aged 6 months to 1 year: serve a small portion of the pudding from beneath the meringue.

Two Layer Lemon Pudding

METRIC/IMPERIAL	AMERICAN
50 g/2 oz butter	*¼ cup butter*
100 g/4 oz sugar	*½ cup sugar*
3 tablespoons lemon juice	*3 tablespoons lemon juice*
1 teaspoon grated lemon rind	*1 teaspoon grated zest of lemon*
50 g/2 oz semolina	*⅓ cup semolina*
2 eggs, separated	*2 eggs, separated*
450 ml/¾ pint milk	*2 cups milk*

Melt the butter in a saucepan, then stir in the sugar, lemon juice and rind. Continue heating until the sugar has dissolved. Stir in the semolina, then beat in the yolks. Add the milk, beating until smooth.

Beat the egg whites until stiff and fold them into the semolina mixture. Transfer to a greased ovenproof dish. Stand the dish in a pan of hot water and bake in a preheated moderate oven (190°C/375°F, Gas Mark 5) for about 30 minutes. Serve either hot or cold.

For babies aged 6 months to 1 year: mash some of the pudding with a little boiled milk.

CHOCOLATE AND ORANGE MERINGUE PUDDING, APPLE SAGO CRISP *(page 78)*
(Photograph: National Dairy Council)

Bread and Butter Pudding

METRIC/IMPERIAL
5 thin slices white bread, buttered, and crusts removed
25 g/1 oz sugar
1 tablespoon drinking chocolate
450 ml/¾ pint milk
2 eggs, beaten

AMERICAN
5 thin slices white bread, buttered, and crusts removed
2 tablespoons sugar
1 tablespoon chocolate powder
2 cups milk
2 eggs, beaten

Cut the bread and butter into squares and lay them, buttered side up, in a greased 900 ml/1½ pint/4 cup ovenproof dish. Sprinkle the bread with sugar. Mix the drinking chocolate with a little milk. Add the remaining milk to the eggs and beat well. Combine with the chocolate mixture and pour over the bread. Bake in a preheated moderate oven (180°C/350°F, Gas Mark 4) for 30 to 35 minutes or until set.

Apple Sago Crisp

METRIC/IMPERIAL
900 ml/1½ pints milk
40 g/1½ oz small pearl sago
25 g/1 oz butter
50 g/2 oz fresh breadcrumbs
25 g/1 oz demerara sugar
⅛ teaspoon powdered cinnamon
225 g/8 oz cooking apples, peeled, cored and sliced

AMERICAN
3¾ cups milk
3 tablespoons pearl sago
2 tablespoons butter
1 cup fresh breadcrumbs
2 tablespoons light brown sugar
⅛ teaspoon powdered cinnamon
½ lb baking apples, peeled, cored and sliced

Heat the milk in a saucepan until almost boiling. Sprinkle the sago in, stir well and simmer gently for 10 minutes, stirring occasionally.

Melt the butter in a saucepan; add the breadcrumbs, sugar and cinnamon and fry gently, turning occasionally, until the breadcrumbs are lightly browned.

Arrange the apples in a buttered ovenproof dish. Pour the sago over, then sprinkle the crumb mixture over the top.

Bake in a preheated moderate oven (160°C/325°F, Gas Mark 3) for 30 minutes or until the apple is tender.

For babies aged 6 months to 1 year: mash a small serving of the pudding to a fairly smooth consistency.

IDEAS FOR TEA

Sandwiches

Rolled Sandwiches
Use thin slices of soft, moist bread and remove the crusts. Only creamy fillings are suitable, for example those made with a butter, margarine or cream cheese base. Spread the filling evenly over the bread and roll up like a Swiss (jelly) roll. Secure with a cocktail stick if necessary. If liked, dip the ends of the sandwich in freshly chopped parsley or Parmesan cheese.

Pinwheel Sandwiches
Slice a sandwich (unsliced) loaf lengthways. Make a long rolled sandwich as described above. Wrap in foil and chill for at least 30 minutes in the refrigerator. When required, cut into 1 cm/½ inch thick rounds.
Note: to make a rolled sandwich roll up more easily, flatten each slice of bread with a rolling pin before spreading with the filling.

Ribbon Sandwiches
Use alternate layers of white and brown bread, one on top of another, with different creamy fillings in between. Remove the crusts. Make a pile of 6 slices of bread, then wrap in foil and chill for 30 minutes. When required, cut into 1 cm/½ inch slices, vertically.

Chequerboard Sandwiches
Pile up ribbon sandwiches as above, using creamy fillings in between each layer and making sure that brown and white breads alternate. Press the stack together; wrap in foil and chill. When required, cut in 1 cm/½ inch slices.

Mosaic Sandwiches
Make sandwiches with 2 slices of either white or brown bread. With a biscuit (cookie) cutter, cut the centre out of each sandwich. Then change round the cut-outs, so the white sandwich has a brown shape in the middle, and the brown sandwich has a white one.

Sandwich Fillings

Cheese and Chives Spread

METRIC/IMPERIAL

50 g/2 oz butter or margarine
1 tablespoon boiling water
100 g/4 oz Cheddar cheese, finely grated
1/2 teaspoon freshly chopped chives

AMERICAN

1/4 cup butter or margarine
1 tablespoon boiling water
1 cup finely grated Cheddar cheese
1/2 teaspoon freshly chopped chives

Cream the butter or margarine with the boiling water. Blend in the cheese and chives. If you wish, substitute blue cheese for Cheddar and omit the chives.

Smoked Cod's Roe Spread

METRIC/IMPERIAL

50 g/2 oz butter or margarine
1 tablespoon boiling water
50 g/2 oz smoked cod's roe, skinned and chopped
1/2 teaspoon lemon juice

AMERICAN

1/4 cup butter or margarine
1 tablespoon boiling water
2 oz smoked cod's roe, skinned and chopped
1/2 teaspoon lemon juice

Cream the butter or margarine with the boiling water. Blend in the roe and lemon juice, mixing very well to make as smooth a spread as possible.

Egg Spread

METRIC/IMPERIAL

50 g/2 oz butter or margarine
1 tablespoon boiling water
2 hard-boiled eggs, chopped

AMERICAN

1/4 cup butter or margarine
1 tablespoon boiling water
2 hard-boiled eggs, chopped

Cream the butter or margarine with the boiling water, then blend in the eggs.

MOSAIC, ROLLED, PINWHEEL AND RIBBON SANDWICHES
(page 79)
(Photograph: Hovis Limited)

Chocolate Spread

METRIC/IMPERIAL	AMERICAN
50 g/2 oz butter or margarine	*¼ cup butter or margarine*
1 tablespoon boiling water	*1 tablespoon boiling water*
4 tablespoons cocoa powder	*¼ cup unsweetened cocoa*
2 tablespoons condensed milk	*2 tablespoons condensed milk*
1 tablespoon black treacle	*1 tablespoon molasses*

Cream the butter or margarine with the boiling water, then blend in the remaining ingredients.

Quick Liver Pâté

METRIC/IMPERIAL	AMERICAN
100 g/4 oz liver sausage	*¼ lb liver sausage*
50 g/2 oz soft margarine	*¼ cup soft margarine*
50 g/2 oz cream cheese	*¼ cup cream cheese*
1 tablespoon single cream	*1 tablespoon light cream*
1 teaspoon lemon juice	*1 teaspoon lemon juice*

Blend all the ingredients together thoroughly.

Tomato Shell Eggs

METRIC/IMPERIAL	AMERICAN
2 large tomatoes	*2 large tomatoes*
a little freshly chopped mint	*a little freshly chopped mint*
2 medium (grade 4) eggs	*2 eggs*

Wipe the tomatoes and cut a 'lid' from the bottom of each. Scoop out the seeds and centre with a teaspoon. Turn the tomatoes upside down on a board and leave to drain.

Put a little mint into each tomato and stand them in a small ovenproof dish. Break the eggs into the tomatoes. Put the 'lids' on top and bake in a preheated moderately hot oven (200°C/400°F, Gas Mark 6) for about 15 minutes, until the tomatoes are beginning to soften and the eggs are just set. Serve with 'soldiers' of bread and butter.

Serves 2 children

Not suitable for babies under 1 year old

Summer Pâté

METRIC/IMPERIAL	AMERICAN
100 g/4 oz soft herring roes	*1/4 lb soft herring roes*
50 g/2 oz butter	*1/4 cup butter*
2 teaspoons lemon juice	*2 teaspoons lemon juice*
2 teaspoons freshly chopped parsley	*2 teaspoons freshly chopped parsley*

Gently fry the roes in half the butter for 10 minutes. Turn into a bowl and pound to a fine paste with a wooden spoon. Soften the remaining butter and add to the roe paste with the lemon juice and parsley. Mix until thoroughly combined.

For babies aged 6 months to 1 year: spread on thinly sliced brown bread. Trim the crusts and cut into tiny squares.

For children over 1 year old: spread on fingers of toast or brown bread (no extra butter is needed).

Tomato Cases

METRIC/IMPERIAL
2 large tomatoes
50 g/2 oz hard and soft herring roes, mixed
15 g/½ oz butter
little Worcestershire sauce
25 g/1 oz Cheddar cheese, grated

AMERICAN
2 large tomatoes
2 oz hard and soft herring roes, mixed
1 tablespoon butter
little Worcestershire sauce
¼ cup grated Cheddar cheese

Cut a thick slice from the top of the tomatoes. Carefully scoop out the flesh, using a teaspoon. Lightly fry the roes in butter, then mix with the tomato pulp and a dash of Worcestershire sauce. Fill the tomato cases with this mixture and top with a little grated cheese. Bake in a preheated moderate oven (180°C/350°F, Gas Mark 4) for 20 minutes.
For babies aged 6 months to 1 year: purée the roe with some tomato flesh and uncooked grated cheese.
For children over 1 year old: serve with fingers of toast.
Serves 2 children

Cheese and Tomato Whirls

METRIC/IMPERIAL
225 g/8 oz self-raising flour
50 g/2 oz butter
100 g/4 oz Gouda cheese, finely grated
4 tablespoons milk
1 egg
Filling:
2 tablespoons tomato purée
75 g/3 oz Gouda cheese, grated

AMERICAN
2 cups self-rising flour
¼ cup butter
1 cup finely grated Gouda cheese
¼ cup milk
1 egg
Filling:
2 tablespoons tomato paste
¾ cup grated Gouda cheese

Sift the flour into a bowl and rub in the butter. Mix in the cheese. Add the beaten milk and egg, reserving a little. Mix to form a soft dough. Roll out into an oblong, approximately 35 × 18 cm/14 x 7 inches. Spread with the tomato purée (paste), leaving a margin on the long sides. Sprinkle with the grated cheese. Brush the margins with the remaining egg mixture. Roll up lengthways as for a Swiss (jelly) roll. Cut into 16 pieces 2 cm/¾ inch thick. Place on a baking sheet and bake in a preheated hot oven (220°C/425°F, Gas Mark 7) for 20 minutes.
Not suitable for babies under 1 year old

SHORTBREAD COOKIES *(page 87)*
(Photograph: McDougalls)

Peter ran straight away to Mr. McGregor's garden, and squeezed under the gate!
he ate some lettuces and some French beans; and then he ate some

All-in-one Victoria Sandwich (Layer Cake)

METRIC/IMPERIAL	AMERICAN
100 g/4 oz self-raising flour	*1 cup self-rising flour*
1 teaspoon baking powder	*1 teaspoon baking soda*
100 g/4 oz soft margarine	*½ cup soft margarine*
100 g/4 oz caster sugar	*½ cup sugar*
2 large eggs	*2 large eggs*
To finish:	**To finish:**
2 tablespoons jam	*2 tablespoons jelly*
1 tablespoon icing sugar	*1 tablespoon confectioners' sugar*

Sift together the flour and baking powder (soda) and place with all the cake ingredients in a bowl. Beat with a wooden spoon until well mixed, light and glossy (2 to 3 minutes) or beat in an electric mixer for 1 minute. Turn the batter into 2 greased and lined 18 cm/7 inch sandwich tins (layer cake pans) or one 20 cm/8 inch sandwich tin (layer cake pan). Smooth the top(s). Bake on the middle shelf of a preheated moderate oven (160°C/325°F, Gas Mark 3). Bake the two 18 cm/7 inch cakes for 25 to 35 minutes, the 20 cm/8 inch cake for 35 to 40 minutes. Turn out and cool on a wire tray. When cold, split the 20 cm/8 inch cake in half. Sandwich the cakes together with jam (jelly) and dust the top with icing (confectioners') sugar.

Chocolate Buns
Follow the basic recipe above, but add 1 tablespoon cocoa (unsweetened cocoa) dissolved in 2 tablespoons boiling water. Turn the batter into 20 paper cases placed on a baking sheet. Bake in a preheated moderately hot oven (190°C/375°F, Gas Mark 5) on the second shelf from the top, for 15 to 20 minutes.

Cherry Cakes
Follow the basic recipe above, but add an extra 25 g/1 oz/¼ cup flour. Turn the batter into 20 paper cases placed on a baking sheet. Press 1 glacé (candied) cherry into each cake. Bake in preheated moderately hot oven (190°C/375°F, Gas Mark 5) on the second shelf from the top, for 15 to 20 minutes.

Frosted Ring Cake
Follow the basic recipe above, but add the finely grated rind of ½ lemon or ½ orange. Bake in a greased and floured 20-22 cm/8-9 inch ring mould. Coat with frosting and decorate with crystallized (candied) lemon or orange slices.

Scotch Pancakes

METRIC/IMPERIAL	AMERICAN
225 g/8 oz self-raising flour	*2 cups self-rising flour*
1 egg	*1 egg*
300 ml/½ pint milk	*1¼ cups milk*

Sift the flour into a bowl. Make a well in the centre and add the egg. Gradually add half the milk, beating well until smooth. Gently stir in the remaining milk. Lightly grease a heavy-based frying pan (skillet) or griddle, and heat until moderately hot. Drop tablespoonfuls of the mixture, well apart, into the pan and cook until bubbles appear on the surface and the underneath is golden brown. Turn over and cook the other side. Wrap in a clean tea towel or absorbent paper and keep warm. Repeat until all the batter is used. Serve warm, spread with butter.

Variations:
For Lemon Pancakes: add 1 teaspoon finely grated lemon rind and 50 g/2 oz/¼ cup caster sugar.
For Cheese Pancakes: add 50 g/2 oz/½ cup finely grated Cheddar cheese and a pinch of mixed herbs.

Shortbread Cookies

METRIC/IMPERIAL	AMERICAN
150 g/6 oz plain flour	*1½ cups all-purpose flour*
100 g/4 oz butter	*½ cup butter*
50 g/2 oz caster sugar	*¼ cup sugar*
50 g/2 oz chocolate, melted, for decoration	*2 squares semi-sweet chocolate, melted, for decoration*

Sift the flour into a bowl and rub in the butter until the mixture resembles breadcrumbs. Mix in the sugar, then knead the mixture until it forms a pliable dough. Divide the dough into 16 pieces and roll each into a ball the size of a walnut. Place on a greased baking tray and flatten each with a fork dipped in cold water. Bake in a pre-heated moderate oven (160°C/325°F, Gas Mark 3) for 15 to 20 minutes. When cold, drizzle thin lines of melted chocolate over the cookies at right angles to the fork lines.

Christmas Cookies

METRIC/IMPERIAL	AMERICAN
100 g/4 oz butter or soft margarine	*½ cup butter or soft margarine*
175 g/6 oz sugar	*¾ cup sugar*
grated rind of 1 orange or lemon	*grated zest of 1 orange or lemon*
2 egg yolks	*2 egg yolks*
225 g/8 oz plain flour	*2 cups all-purpose flour*
1 teaspoon baking powder	*1 teaspoon baking soda*

Beat the butter or margarine with the sugar and grated rind until the mixture is light and fluffy. Add the egg yolks. Sift together the flour and baking powder (soda) and mix all the ingredients together to make a firm dough. Lightly knead the dough until it is smooth, then roll out very thinly on a floured surface. Cut into fancy shapes with biscuit (cookie) cutters and transfer carefully to greased baking sheets. (If you wish to hang the cookies, as shown in the picture opposite, make a small hole in the top of each with a skewer.) Bake the cookies in a preheated moderate oven (180°C/350°F, Gas Mark 4) for 6 to 8 minutes.

To decorate the biscuits, make up a little glacé icing with icing (confectioners') sugar and water, just stiff enough to drop from a spoon. Divide into separate small dishes and colour each portion with a drop of food colouring. Use a small piping bag fitted with a writing nozzle to decorate the cookies with icing.

Decorations may be applied while the icing is still wet.

Peanut Cookies

METRIC/IMPERIAL	AMERICAN
150 g/5 oz soft margarine	*⅔ cup soft margarine*
100 g/4 oz crunchy peanut butter	*¼ lb crunchy peanut butter*
150 g/5 oz granulated sugar	*⅔ cup white sugar*
100 g/4 oz soft brown sugar	*⅔ cup light brown sugar*
1 egg, beaten	*1 egg, beaten*
½ teaspoon vanilla essence	*½ teaspoon vanilla extract*
150 g/5 oz self-raising flour	*1¼ cups self-rising flour*

Cream the margarine, peanut butter and sugars together until light and fluffy. Beat in the egg and vanilla essence (extract) and then stir in flour. Roll the mixture into walnut-sized pieces and place them well apart on a greased baking sheet. Flatten the cookies with a floured fork and bake in a preheated moderate oven (180°C/350°F, Gas Mark 4) for 10 to 12 minutes.

CHRISTMAS COOKIES
(Photograph: McDougalls)

So Light
So Fine
McDougalls
Flour

Hedgehog Cake

METRIC/IMPERIAL	AMERICAN
1 Victoria sandwich cake, see recipe page 86	*1 Victoria layer cake, see recipe page 86*
50 g/2 oz chocolate matchsticks	*2 oz chocolate matchsticks*
small sweets for the eyes and nose	*small candies for the eyes and nose*
Chocolate frosting:	**Chocolate frosting:**
2 tablespoons cocoa powder	*2 tablespoons unsweetened cocoa*
2 tablespoons hot water	*2 tablespoons hot water*
75 g/3 oz soft margarine	*1/3 cup soft margarine*
225 g/8 oz icing sugar, sifted	*2 cups confectioners' sugar, sifted*

To make the frosting: blend the cocoa with the hot water; add the margarine and icing (confectioners') sugar and beat well.

Cut the cake in half, to make 2 semi-circles. Sandwich the halves together with a little of the frosting. Trim one end for the nose and face. Spread the frosting all over the cake. Using a palette knife, smooth the face and swirl the frosting over the body. Cover the body with chocolate matchsticks to represent spines. Use the sweets (candies) to represent the eyes and nose.

Malt Bread

METRIC/IMPERIAL	AMERICAN
225 g/8 oz self-raising flour	*2 cups self-rising flour*
1 teaspoon bicarbonate of soda	*1 teaspoon baking soda*
150 ml/1/4 pint milk	*2/3 cup milk*
2 tablespoons malt extract	*2 tablespoons malt extract*
2 tablespoons golden syrup	*2 tablespoons light corn syrup*
1 egg, beaten	*1 egg, beaten*
100 g/4 oz sultanas	*2/3 cup seedless white raisins*

Sift the flour and soda into a bowl. Place the milk, malt extract and syrup in a saucepan and heat gently, stirring until blended. Add the syrup mixture and the egg to the flour, and beat until smooth. Stir in the sultanas (raisins). Pour the mixture into a greased and lined 500 g/1 lb loaf tin (pan). Bake in a preheated moderately hot oven (190°C/375°F, Gas Mark 5) for 45 to 50 minutes.

INDEX

79/555